A

BOOK

OF

LIFE

A BOOK OF LIFE

PETER KINGSLEY

A BOOK OF LIFE

First published in 2021 by
Catafalque Press, London
www.catafalquepress.com
contact@catafalquepress.com

ISBN 978-1-9996384-4-3 (hardcover)
ISBN 978-1-9996384-5-0 (paperback)

Front cover painting:
Pond 6 by Neville Sattentau
www.nevart.co.uk

Book design by Leslie Bartlett
www.lesliebartlett.com

British Library Cataloguing in Publication Data
A catalogue record for this book is
available from the British Library

ΠΑΥΡΟΝ ΔΕ ΖΩΗΙϹΙ
ΒΙΟΥ ΜΕΡΟϹ
ΑΘΡΗϹΑΝΤΕϹ

ONE

SEEDING

1

P L E A S E be very careful of this book.

Watch out. Don't trust it for a moment or take the slightest thing for granted.

Take enough time to get to know it. And far better, give it all the time it needs so it can get to know you.

Watch the things you say in its presence. Start treating it with respect so that it might even come to respect you. Learn that what you feel about it is of no significance compared to whatever it might feel about you as it reads and notes your every thought, registering your hesitations.

Let me explain.

This book has a life and an intelligence of its own. Or to be a little more precise, each chapter is a conscious being. Their words are nothing but the crustings sometimes attached to a creature's back: not the whole story by any means.

And honestly, to be quite truthful, this book has been written to be read—but not by you.

To write it, I had to be taken to a place so terrifyingly deep I no longer even existed as a human being. And to read it and understand it, the same would have to happen to you.

By some strangely mysterious process we've come to believe books are written by humans and for humans to read. That's not at all how it started out or the way these things were meant to be.

But bit by bit, when everybody's back was turned, that's how it ended up. Every trace of consciousness was crushed by the endless weight of lifeless words and the arteries of the world got so blocked up, no living being even knows how to breathe properly any more.

And this is all because we forgot. And we forgot that we'd forgotten. And then we forgot we'd forgotten that there was anything to forget. Totally lost was any memory of the timeless, headless beings who line the beaches as our protectors.

We no longer remembered the gods.

But that's not to say I, or this book, am inviting you to remember. It's far too late for any of that.

When we're masking our forgetfulness: that's when we're being asked to remember. When suddenly we long to wake up, that's because it's already too late.

It's not at all what sometimes is said, that the clock's ticking close to midnight. To wake up means waking up to the fact that it already passed the point of midnight several days ago.

And so these words are not for you now, because there's no now left to speak of. They're no more meant for you than life is, than the birds are singing just for you.

They're not so much a book as an unbook that keeps intact by staying unread.

This is a depository of seeds saved for a dim and distant future, destined for those who don't yet exist or for those who exist no longer. And if you are stuck between the two, feel quite free to watch as a witness: to look like innocent passers-by.

To be sure, without a single doubt, this book will take you back all the way to the source of life—if you allow it. All you have to do is let the words fall silent like the rain inside you.

They'll take care of the rest, as this is the rarest of things: a book of life.

2

I WAIT HERE at the edge of this book like rocks on the edge of the ocean.

One chapter could take a thousand years, less or plus some centuries here and there. Writer or reader makes no difference: we're not the ones who make things happen. To live, do, breathe in, die, sing some song, we all need the mercy of the sea.

In the language of the Lakota I am known as Heyoka. I break, just as I'm doing right now, whatever others are too frightened to break even though they know the time has come. I do this just as I'm required to because I'm the Contrary, the clown.

I come, then I go, when others stay; stay put long after they've disappeared. I know how to say words that all the military might or might-not of the People's Republic of America or United States of China would never find the courage to say. I break up from the depths far below the soul only to turn straight away—waiting, waiting so patiently, for the tides of eternity to change.

My dance is different from the others' and I have colours beyond belief. I have no interest at all in the rubbish people gather because I remember the treasures that they lost.

I say the secrets others wish would go away. When they talk I go silent, as the only words I can make out are the language of wind or birds.

They laugh, I cry. And I collapse at the comedy of their pomposity, their astonishing flights of rightness. I fight for what they find quite futile; but when they fight, I walk away.

And I walk in the other direction, backwards, always by different ways, because thanks to this powerlessness I'm obliged to be the balance for everybody else's acts and words.

There's more that could be said, much more that should be said in better times than these.

In the older traditions of the Cherokee I am one of those who dance on the left of the sky people.

Never taught to dance like the living I don't dance with them, won't dance for them. Face painted white, I dance for the dead. Skull-faced, I am the dead I dance for.

I'm a dancer for the Ancestors: for those who have never been buried, those whose names no one can quite recall, the ones they thought they could do without.

And it's so strange, so infinitely strange, to see how people who speak my language don't have a clue what I mean or the slightest sense of what I do.

I've travelled around and around and, it's very true, many times I found the faintest trace of recognition there or there: small stirrings that pulse from the distantly thudding memory of who we are and why we are here, a hollow in the brain, a bleeding deep inside the body, a seizure because something's coming together.

But most are so eager to forget, it's over the moment it started. Only a year or day or second later and they've already passed on—frantically searching for the next trick, still stunned from the superhuman strain of trying just for once to remember.

And the pale faces are back, cold, hard, with their proud dreams of evolution and blanketed expressions that say: Do not enter here, leave me in peace, let me dance with my nightmares alone.

Now the darkness is gathering quickly like so many times before. Even the raw sunlight is no longer real. Left to their devices, humans can't help inventing ever better scenes of devastation—entire cultures bent on uprooting their own nature, scared to death of their own sacredness.

So it's high time I, too, start to dance.

I dance with words instead of bodies: these words. There's a true dance to be told about the human and the divine, about time and the timeless, but not for the sake of shaking people up. If they wished, they'd be awake by now.

They are not the ones who need waking.

WESTERN CIVILIZATION is the tenderest plant imaginable, even more fragile than human life.

It was brought, perfect, from far away—just like every other culture that has existed or that will exist. Then it was planted, tended, watered by the line of beings who brought it.

Civilizations don't just happen, don't simply appear out of nowhere. There would never be a single thing without the sowers, planters, farmers who bring their seeds from another world only to deposit them in this.

I am in the lineage of those who fetched this western world into being. Each one of these words arrives straight from the very same place it once came from.

But this is no time for creating, for helping life to blossom or bloom. What then was planted is hopelessly overgrown, has totally gone to seed; and the great time for clearing has come.

Winds of fear are sweeping through the world. Most people fight hard not to notice. Others are so scared they get violent. All the rest, they just tremble like leaves.

Wisdom always treasures clean endings, which so sadly are my expertise. And hope is such a poor substitute for the intensity of utter hopelessness which right now is needed.

Holding back the tears isn't easy. But the only way to face the fear is to return to the root of this civilization, is to go back to the darkness where it all began.

I know all this because I am it. I breathe with the sowers of this world; carry with me in my belly their original instructions for how to live wisely in the world they sowed. And each day I speak to the people still living inside it through its trees, its sky, through the cries of its creatures.

It's the same old story as always. In every sacred tradition the secret is not to belong to it, but to become it instead. This is nothing special. It's just a matter of being in harmony with nature.

Honestly there's little left of me now, aside of course from foolishness. My story's the story of this world. By being told, we both fade away until there's nothing left of either.

Keep an eye on me: you'll see the truth at the heart of your own existence. I'm what's awake behind your senses. Look up—I'm the colour of your sky.

Hear me sing to you through the bird song and for the first time you'll hear the birds singing simply and sweetly for you.

SPROUTING

4

Nothing comes anywhere close to the experience of becoming human.

To discover we're not this two-legged body is unbelievably easy: is the simplest thing one could do. Children can be taught it, ought to have been taught it, in school.

But the senseless spells recited for centuries by spiritual and scientific authorities have been more than enough to leave everyone dizzy, disoriented, lost.

The consciousness behind our body is what's looking out through the eyes right now, listening moment to moment through the ears. And it never changes, is never born, never dies.

Death and birth and all the other fidgetings of change take place inside it. The trouble is that unless you've learned how to ease yourself into the saddle of consciousness, life will throw you as soon as it can and knock you out.

Anyone who identifies with the body while alive will identify with it when it dies. And that's the end of their story. But whoever stays alive while the body dies instead of going unconscious realizes how much has been lost—knows at first hand what it means to be a human and sees the purpose of the body and understands how necessary it is.

It's heavy and blunt, impossibly limiting, unbearably dumb. But without it there are certain things that in a whole eternity can never be done.

Whoever remembered for one second the pain of trying to speak without a voice or to love without a body, to reach and touch, remind and guide, to help in setting things right, wouldn't be able to waste another moment of the life that's been given. From then on, everything is urgency all the time.

A human life is so incredibly rare and precious that there are those who wait thousands of years just for the hope of a single chance. It's not the kind of thing to take lightly or throw away.

As the old, wise saying goes: A life in the hand is worth two in the bush.

And it's so unimaginably fragile.

Life as a human is this—to walk out into the open fields of existence with a sniper behind every bush, snipers of sickness and forgetfulness and death. Some manage to take thirty steps, others seventy or eighty; a few don't even make twenty or ten.

If people only recognized how fragile it is, this short-lived gift of human life, they would all get together and plan how to live consciously and honourably: how not to fritter their time away in making war or money or even in making children.

But they won't because they can't. And they can't because this is one of the best kept secrets—that people are not yet human.

They think they must be, pretend to themselves and to others that they are. Grown women and men put on airs of being accomplished human beings just like tiny seeds claiming to be a tree.

Children are fresh seeds. Old people are shrivelled seeds. Spiritual people, artistic people, very clever people all lie somewhere in the spectrum between wrinkled and smooth.

But this culture never even got as far as the sprouting.

Most people don't want, of course, to hear that they aren't what they're meant to be. Only a few, the smallest handful, are willing and ready to listen—except that wanting or not wanting doesn't make the slightest bit of difference.

Either way, all people know it in their hearts.

This is the darkest secret inside their closet: the unspoken knowledge, tucked so well away out of sight, that nothing from birth through to death is ever what it seems.

And human life is the mystery that's silently waiting to be lived.

TREASURE the time when your parents die.

If you are lucky enough to be able to stand or sit alone beside the dead body of a mother, of a father, you just might have a chance to glimpse the total joke of it all.

Maybe you'll realize how unbelievably ridiculous it is to enter physical existence through the bodies of two human beings and, like some back-to-front magician, transform freedom into utter dependency inside a world of bodies and things.

All of a sudden you're having to beg for what you are— rely on lumbering adults for nourishment and comfort and warmth, on unpredictable circumstances for protection and love and support. What used to be infinitely present, not the tiniest need for grasping or snatching with the fingers of any hand, now hangs by the thinnest thread from a yes or no.

That's inside the first cluster of surprises on the path of becoming human.

There are many other shocks along the way. In fact it invisibly consists of shock upon shock. And needed the body may be—absolutely indispensable. But that's not to say the moment won't come when all the needs of existence have to be left aside because another necessity is calling.

As with everything in nature, it's simply a matter of being ready for the next turn at the right time.

My parents already had two daughters. For him that was enough but she longed for a son. So she did the obvious thing and seduced him when he was half asleep.

And she got what she wanted. But, as so often happens when we're given what we ask for, she ended up with a little more than expected.

It can be a bit unnerving to have a baby who tells you without words what to do. I was very particular about how she should take care of me. With her experience as a professional photographer she knew how to create a dark room and made one just for me. The only other people allowed inside were my two sisters, provided they sat quietly in complete silence as she fed me—nourished, from the start, by the prayerfulness of women.

To survive, really survive, we all need some magic thread through the chaos of existence that's different from every other thread which snaps or binds. Mine was prayer: not the empty and pretentious formalities invented by men when the life has already left them, but something else.

The reality was going out and kneeling in nature, feeling the gracefulness all around but also the weight of the sky on my back—because even as a child I knew how expensive it is to become human.

The cost is your own being: is agreeing to be turned inside out until you emerge as an object inside the world that's inside the universe that you are.

The price is having to look up at the stars and wonder if perhaps there might be life up there—the absurdest of questions considering how you are the light of the stars looking down on yourself.

Prayer, in its essence, is nothing like what it's usually seen as: submission to some divinity bigger than one is. It's simply to quiet the small body and focus the even smaller self until they merge back into that vaster self they come from.

So often, I've noticed just how natural prayer and a prayerful attitude are for little children. They love the ebb and flow of life pulsing through their bodies, carrying them back and forward in a matter of seconds between what they've become and what they are.

In my case it was kneeling in the grass that worked best, palms flat together, eyes closed, sometimes even a prostration, the faintest of smiles.

The stalks bent by knees and shins would rise up inside me, tickle the belly, grow into my being. They talked with their strong green voices.

They took me back to where I began.

A LITTLE after I learned to walk I was given a railway engine.

It was wooden, painted, with a string attached. My great adventure of the day was taking the two steep steps down from the kitchen door and guiding it one way, then back, on the narrow passage that ran beside our home.

A pair of metal garbage bins, one a little shorter than the other, were standing outside the kitchen window halfway along the alley. Often I'd slow down to look up at them with affection as they loomed over me like two battered giants, while the train and I went by.

And here—between the black cast-iron gate at one end and a glimpse of garden at the other—was my best time, my free time, my real time. This was time for contemplation and for going to school: the only school, on reflection, where I ever learned a single genuine thing.

I was pupil. I was teacher. And, yes, I was the lesson to be learned.

As I walked up and down with the engine rolling behind me, I summarized what I knew in the simplest form I could manage; condensed it into its essence; laid it out for view. And this is what I'd say to myself with the voice I'd always had:

Now you're a little person with engine and string. But look at what's looking; listen to what's listening. What's watching through your eyes and hearing the sounds around you and smelling air and sensing the breeze isn't little or big. It isn't young. It isn't old. It's what it always has been and always will be.

Your body will grow bigger and taller until eventually it's as large as your parents' or all those peculiar adults'. But this that you are, that's seeing and hearing and aware of everything moving and changing around you: it never grows and never moves. It never has changed. It never can change. It never will.

Even when you've become a gigantic adult like the others, this that you are won't have altered at all. It will be just as fresh, then, as in this moment—exactly the same. And you'll remember it then just as you know it now because only when you know this, only when you are it, does everything make sense.

Each time, outside with myself, was always the same time. Every day, what was watching the clouds rush by or suddenly felt the sun come out from behind them was telling itself it would never change. And this conscious demonstration, this unending reminder of what I'd known since the beginning of time, reverberated so deeply and spread so far through my little body that it could no more be forgotten than I could forget myself.

Anyone a little inexperienced in these things might very naturally say how wonderful it must have been for a small child to enjoy such constant clarity—except that the reality couldn't have been more different.

It was hell.

Slowly learning to talk was, for me, the opportunity to start sharing and speaking about this. The only trouble is, that wasn't what people were looking to hear. Before I said anything, they'd be all smiles and childish noises. But the moment I began framing some words for them, their jaws would lock. Their eyeballs started twisting and turning in their sockets.

And, as I began to understand, it wasn't just that no one wanted to hear.

It was that no one could afford to hear, because the whole adult world is built on the denial—on the infantile defiance—of this.

Loneliness became as ever-present as the awareness. Between the birthday parties and the special treats, life meant trying to find some trick to help get by with lunatics who have created a fantasy world for themselves.

To be playing innocently with toys and at the same time observing that everyone is asleep, seeing the excruciating meaninglessness of their existence, can be too heavy a burden for any child to bear. And what I hadn't discovered yet was that there are three types of humans, or human destinies.

The first type is the person who never wakes up. If it's a viable option, this is highly recommended.

The second is the usual case of people who are going to start waking up, at the earliest, in their teens or twenties. This is extremely convenient. It allows time for building a body and personality and ego which will be fully in tune with the unconsciousness of the world—and which, in spite of what anyone might claim, will always remain mostly unconscious. That's a very sensible compromise, and is also warmly recommended.

Third is the case of someone who has to carry the thread of awareness completely unbroken. In certain situations and circumstances, that can sometimes be needed. But it's a gruesome undertaking.

In this third case, the sensitivity required knows no limits. A subtlety of perception comes with it, a freedom from any convention that can't be matched, an ability to dance or shift shape like trees and leaves in the wind.

At the same time it brings with it a suffering that's unimaginable, as if your own hand is set on fire and plunged inside your innards. It carries a sadness that's boundless, because someone has to experience what every person knows but is too frightened to admit. It hides the unbearable loneliness of all nature crying to be seen or felt or heard: of life being trampled out of existence with every civilized footstep. And it contains deep inside itself the sharp edge of anxiety and confusion which, whatever anyone might like to think, are the unavoidable consequence of incarnating completely.

After all, there's never a true encounter with the sacred that doesn't turn our whole world upside down—that doesn't shake away each little lump of earth underneath our feet.

And sometimes even a small child has to take responsibility for acting as the living intermediary between reality and that world of nightmares others live in; is asked to take pity on the poor people wandering so far from themselves; is shown that somebody must keep conscious so everyone else can stay unconscious, that someone needs to stay on watch while the others sleep and has to go on remembering while they are walking straight out over the cliffs of forgetfulness.

But of course I couldn't say that or show it. The birds knew. The wind knew, the rain knew. The cats knew. They knew that I knew. For a moment, another boy or girl might know before running off the nearest cliff.

And this was the secret of growing up in an empty world. With family, with guests, with friends it was always the same.

I would pose together with our cat beside the electric fireplace.

FRAGRANCE

Ｐｅｏｐｌｅ ｌｏｖｅ hearing all about the lives of others, but never heard that no humans have a life of their own.

Even our joys and sufferings aren't ours. They're being suffered, enjoyed, by those whose existence we hardly ever glimpse—let alone allow into our lives. And what we call one human life is nothing but an optical illusion.

Each apparent continuity from birth to death is a fabricated lie, specks of flying dust on the breathing fabric of infinity.

And that's what matters, only that: to keep pointing back to reality.

Whichever way I turned as a child, every experience or incident or moment was another encounter with the infinite. Their depth was immeasurable, so was their source, so was their significance. And so was the depth of ignorance needed not to notice—because the life behind each single instant knows no bounds.

It was a constant struggle to try convincing myself I was someone separate from everything else. I was the shirt

I wore, the pattern on the blanket, the ball bouncing on the concrete. If I won at sports, I was the loser.

I was the thief in the news, the beggar on the street. At times it was so bad, I had to make up little rituals to remind myself of my identity and my name.

But how people could be satisfied with just one body was beyond me when there was so much beauty, so much mystery, beyond and outside.

The small street we lived on in suburban London was lined with trees. Coming home from school I'd run zigzag across the road—infuriating the neighbours in their little cars—because I needed to greet them all.

But aside from nature I only knew endless aloneness. Even the kindest of people gestured and jumped like puppets on a string. There was no point or purpose to human existence, nothing to live for, no one real; and those who were most pompous in their purposefulness were the hollowest of all.

Then, one day, everything changed.

It's strange to see how certain events exert an effect on the time before, just as much as on the time that comes after. Sometimes we wait without sensing what we're waiting for or even being aware of the waiting. But that waiting is what makes our breaths, what shapes everything we are and do.

And all I knew as the years circled round was that something essential was missing.

Each afternoon as I came back from school was pretty much the usual story. I'd take a slice of bread with a little jam upstairs to my bedroom and sit down to do some homework.

But one day—I can't have been much older than ten or eleven—everything seemed the same as always. And nothing was the same.

I climbed the stairs I knew so well with plate in one hand, satchel in the other. I fiddled with the doorknob, turned it, walked into my room and was stunned by what I saw.

Every tiniest detail was the way it always would be: bed and headboard, basin in the corner, curtains pulled back. The small window was slightly open above the main one. But there was something else that made me put down the plate on the chest of drawers, drop my satchel in amazement.

Someone was in the room, waiting for me. As soon as I came in, he gathered himself and moved across to the open window and was gone.

I saw this all as clearly and distinctly as I'd ever seen anything. And with my eyes I saw absolutely nothing.

That was startling enough. But what made the situation immeasurably stranger was the total sense of familiarity that swept over me the moment he left. I knew precisely what had happened without the slightest visible sign.

Someone had been visiting to check on me, see how I was living and take good note of my surroundings, observe how I was coming along. This unphysical visitor was the watcher of my life and experience: had always been caring for me, looking after me with a timeless patience no human parent could ever hope to match.

This time, he was just so gently pleased I'd noticed. It had only taken the softest nudge and I remembered.

Suddenly I realized that I'd never been alone; and if your wisdom tempts you to think this was nothing but a fictitious compensation by some young boy for his solitary existence, you don't understand that all our wise existences are nothing but a misguided attempt to compensate for this.

My hands were empty.

All those little things I'd held on to were gone. I sat on the bed, lost in the gap between two realities—shocked by what I'd been shown, staggered that there was nothing at all to show for what had happened.

And then the scent came: started spreading through the room. It grew so powerful, I remember shutting the door because I didn't want the trouble of my mother asking what it was.

Expanding everywhere in perfect silence was the most astonishing fragrance I had ever smelled. I'd never experienced anything even close to it—infinitely more natural than any perfume, as fresh as the freshest flowers but totally different, the fragrance behind all fragrances.

And I knew without a doubt, because the fragrance told me, that this was his signature. This was his calling card for after he'd gone, a parting message of affection to say: yes, the things you saw were real.

It was only about ten years later, riding in a dark bus back to London one night, that I started to discover other people had also had the same experience. Straining to look through some pages from a book I'd just bought, about ancient oracles and prophets, I read how the Greeks and Romans said there was one sure sign of divine presence any visiting god would leave behind.

And this was the extraordinary fragrance that appears as if out of nowhere, spreading everywhere it can.

8

$\mathbb{F}$EW THINGS could sound quite as delightful as having a divine visitor.

But let's just say the reality is a little more complex than that. And it's not all good news, to be sure, because there isn't too much that's as shattering for a human being.

The fragrance that had spread through my room also spread downwards, then outwards, inside me. And I knew—it could hardly have been more obvious even to a child—that there wasn't a thing I could do.

I realized it was hopeless to try getting any closer to what had happened, and refused to get away from it by trying to forget. Instead, I just watched and waited.

Slowly the centre of my consciousness started shifting to where no one in their right mind would ever expect it to be. Any lingering sense of independence was silently, systematically, annihilated. And it began to dawn on me with more clarity than ever before that I'd never be able to take the initiative in anything again.

The ache for an intimacy I'd experienced in the space of several seconds dropped like liquid metal straight into my belly and became a magnet that grew stronger, then stronger, with time.

Sometimes it would pull me through one delightful experience after another so it could show me they were even less than paper-thin—that there was nothing to them, nothing behind them.

Then it would pull me away from everything so it could reveal the whole world as lifeless and flat. Whenever I tried looking outside, instead of in, I'd be crushed by an overwhelming heaviness and sadness until I remembered again. It took quite a while for me to see that most of what goes, among so-called adults, by the name of depression isn't a disease or defect at all.

On the contrary, it's a perfectly natural response to the pull of the divine which is always disturbing and disrupting and disorienting—straining to reorient us towards a totally different dimension. And it's those who seem best adjusted, armed like tragic soldiers with their psychological theories and fanciful facts, who are most helplessly trapped in their strange delusions.

An unstoppable longing became my master. I always had made good efforts to obey all the stated, if not unspoken, rules. But now there was only a single rule I could follow.

I started disappearing whenever possible: just walked away and was gone.

I wandered to the remotest places, found myself in other countries, learned to live without any money, discovered the subtle arts and sciences of hitchhiking which vary so completely from region to region, picked up languages as well as the sound and flow of different dialects so I could speak to people without anybody even thinking to wonder where I came from.

Often I'd visit an old friend who had moved to Germany, talk with him until after midnight, then walk out to a place where I'd start hitchhiking around and around the German motorways sometimes for days.

To me it didn't matter in the slightest where I was going. I simply went where I was taken—without any choice, just accepting whichever car came my way. I knew there was somewhere I needed to go, somewhere I was being drawn to, although I didn't have a clue where it was or how on earth to get from here to there.

So this is the way I travelled: my constant exercise in humility and surrender, the best possible offering of my helplessness. All the time there was the longing, the endless desperateness leading me until I could turn to go home and back to school for a few more weeks or months before being pulled away again.

One summer I was circling around Germany and started getting rides to Villach, down through Ljubljana and Zagreb and Belgrade, then across the north of Greece towards the Turkish border. I met travellers coming the other way who babbled terrifying stories of being ganged up on and attacked by Turks. At first, when I saw a Turkish truck or car approaching, my reaction was to run and hide behind a bush. But by the time I arrived in Istanbul I realized I had to face my fear.

I walked out of the city and, on a small country lane, came across a group of old men sitting under a tree in a field beside the road. They invited me over and we found we could communicate in French. They taught me that physical gestures and body language around Asia are entirely different from in the western world; showed me how to move and gesture with my head; initiated me into Turkish words and language.

I had no idea where I was going. I had no map, had no plan. I had absolutely no curiosity to know where I was: for week after week it never even occurred to me to ask.

All I did was put one foot in front of the other, follow the paths and roads as the magnet drew me up through mountains and around lakes and beside the sea; accept each ride and experience and meeting, the hospitality and hardship, as they came along. All I had was a little blue canvas sailor's bag my uncle had been given during the war that contained a sleeping bag and my passport, a toothbrush along with a change of underwear I would wash with my shirt in the rivers or streams. All I noticed was that my skin kept getting browner in the car mirrors and my Turkish kept getting better.

One late afternoon, an old Mercedes pulled up and a young boy sitting next to the man at the wheel slid over to make space beside them. We were driving through a landscape that made my heart feel it was going to burst. We started dropping into a valley and a voice was singing inside me: You are coming home, you are coming home.

We arrived in a town that stunned me with its dignity and beauty. This time I couldn't help noticing the name on the signs. It was Antakya: Antioch.

I began walking and saw a park ahead. It was early evening and a procession of men on both sides of me, still in their work clothes, were moving towards the park entrance with packets in their hand. They all sat down together on the grass, unwrapped the food they had brought and called me over to join them. Suddenly I was in the middle of a feast as the flowers surrounding us released their perfume.

And every bone of my body knew that I had come home, I had come home.

Home is never where we guess it is.

Whatever we think of as home is just a step along the way. The sweetness of homecoming only marks a stopping place for whoever's ready to be seduced and willing to be tricked—because without experiencing the limits of restlessness you can never discover the stillness beyond any shape or form.

All that night I slept with the roses, but early the next morning I pulled myself from the earth and was gone.

It wasn't too long before I arrived in a breathtakingly beautiful forest. A man in a wooden hut between the trees stamped my passport and soon I was surrounded by the smells, and sights, and sounds of Syria.

Now there was no longer the same feeling of being home. That was all gone, replaced by the sense of being welcomed into the sacred home of homes.

For a while I was taken from city to city. But that turned out to have little significance because what mattered was the spaces in between.

Something else kept drawing me. I found myself being pulled straight out into the blazing heat of the desert with no protection, without even any water: only with a mysterious kind of trust that didn't feel like trust at all because there wasn't the slightest choice involved.

This is the ancient tradition that I didn't even know of at the time.

Once I walked in the middle of the day into the middle of nowhere, nothing but stones and sand wherever I looked. Alone under the brilliant sun I started drifting into and out of unconsciousness, pulled by the magnet, not for a moment caring about anything else. And then by some ridiculously impossible chance—they said it was the will of Allah—I was being rescued by a small group of men who just so happened to see me from a road far away in the distance.

They helped me into their truck and, as they headed into town, everything went entirely black.

When my consciousness finally came back, I couldn't move. The pain everywhere inside the body was unbearable. After a long time I slowly managed to open my eyes to see camels walking upside down, and wondered if this is what they do in the world we go to when we die. But at last I started becoming more aware of my surroundings.

I was lying, face upwards, on a marble slab with my head hanging straight down at one end in the middle of a market place. The loud speaker from a bus station nearby was announcing arrivals, destinations, and I heard I was in Aleppo.

It took a good while, and a good number of adventures, to recover. But as soon as I could, I was gone. And I kept being drawn back towards the desert borderlands where Syria meets Turkey.

One day I was walking out again into the desert. And, again, I didn't care. Nothing would stop me—the pull was so powerful that I would have walked right into the sea if it was in my way.

I followed what seemed like a little old track. And things happened on that walk which I wouldn't even try to write or explain.

After a long time I saw a peculiar pattern ahead in the sand and rock. As I came closer I started to realize what it was. Straight in front of me was a deep winding channel cut into the desert. There were steep banks of sand on either side and a clear, strong river—obviously a tributary—running along the bottom.

I walked up; sat down; stayed sitting, gazing into the water. Time passed. The sun kept moving. And, little by little, the realization started dawning that something had become completely unmoving inside me.

The magnet and its pull were gone. Instead, there was absolute stillness and peace. I was where I had been pulled and dragged to—unbelievably free.

Even home had been left behind, even the home of homes, and there was nowhere to go any more. I'd been returned to my root and source.

Eventually I heard a noise in the distance and looked up. A man was leading a donkey towards the river bank some way off to my left. I didn't move. He brought the donkey to the edge and half pushed it, half kicked it down the steep slope to make it drink.

Then he caught sight of me and clearly couldn't believe what he saw. He started shouting and demanding to know what the hell I was doing. I greeted him politely and told him he should mind his own business. The donkey was quietly drinking.

Next he yelled at me, saying I didn't belong there and insisting I go home. I calmly but firmly told him that I do, and was as much at home as he was—which left him speechless.

Now it was my turn to ask him where we were: what was the name of this water and region. He stared in utter amazement at my ignorance, waved his arm with a sweeping gesture as if embracing the whole wide area, and called out: Furat! Furat!

Without knowing it, I had arrived in the great basin of the Euphrates.

The donkey left along with the man and there was only the silence of the desert. When at last I got up, I knew I would never have to travel in search of anything again. I'd travel for other reasons, of course; but not for that.

And I left. It was to be years before I would come back to this region—to die.

Returning from the Euphrates to England was astonishingly easy and took almost no time at all. But there was one constant impression, whether being driven by an ambassador's car through Turkey or crossing the Alps in a Jaguar at midnight, that overrode everything else.

Travelling from Asia through Europe to London felt exactly like carrying water in a sieve. To hold the living reality of what had happened, out in the deserts of Turkey and Syria, was an absolute impossibility. The patterns of thought, the affluence, the complacency of people and places in Europe all drained away the sacred—very silently, insidiously, but so steadily. And I realized for the first time that certain inner experiences and states can never be carried from place to place in their entirety.

It seems as if they can. The mind with its tiny share of wisdom would love to insist that they can. After all, the traces of memory are still so clear and alive. But the body which is the knower of everything knows otherwise.

And only when we've become conscious of the irrelevance of place, of the reality that even while moving physically our consciousness is never moving an inch, do we become aware of how important place is.

Different parts of the earth affect not only how we talk. They influence who we are and what we're allowed to reach inside ourselves. Sometimes we are lucky enough to be given access to states of awareness that are permanent, that stay unchanging wherever we are and even regardless of whether we're alive or dead.

But the deeper we sink into those states, the more sensitive we become to where we are on the surface of the earth—because some things are simply not transportable.

The earth is a divine being far greater than any ordinary thoughts can fathom. And there are degrees, and there are depths, to the divine impossible to imagine.

It was only years later that I sat down with some maps to retrace my steps and see what I could find about the place where I'd been taken. The result was quite surprising.

At the time, all I had eyes for was the inner reality which is free of any form. That was all I cared for; all I trusted. And in fact the irresistible longing had drawn me to what used to be among the greatest centres of wisdom on earth, poised along the silk road linking Europe to Persia and India and China.

Without any conscious interest or the slightest curiosity on my part, I'd been brought straight to the heart of a land once famous as the hearth of the prophets; as a seat of devotion to the divine nature of the planets; as a crucial source of Gnostic teachings and of the forms Christianity would come to assume when it started spreading out around the world.

But aside from all this is something else, too.

Here was a place where people strained for centuries through persecution, through torture, through death, to preserve intact the philosophical and prophetic traditions of the ancient Greeks so that their essence could eventually be transmitted to the East.

Some of those old Greek prophets and philosophers are still remembered in the West, at least by name. But who

they really were, what they were, what they were doing—
that was forgotten long ago.

And one of them was Empedocles.

Two

LEANINGS

10

Soon, those school days were gone and along came the question of what to do next.

Sometimes it's so easy, in retrospect, to see where life was set on carrying us. But the trickery used to get us from here to there is always breathtaking. And any reality in what seems to be our own life is not ours.

It's simply the reality of what's pulling us.

Ever since I'd performed in a play as a little boy, I was acutely aware everything is only a show. Quite often, young friends were surprised when I'd say all I cared for was being able to slide behind the scenes and disappear.

None of my family had the slightest clue how to do that. Neither did anyone at school, or the strangers I met on my journeys. But I had no doubt that there are those who know how to move right through the senses and emerge on the other side—who have refined the art of weaving into and out of existence at will.

We all have to start here, or there. I started in the north of England by going to study philosophy at a new university where the students were alive and the countryside was wild. It felt necessary, for reasons I couldn't yet fathom, to become acquainted as straightforwardly as possible with the accumulated wisdom of our culture.

And to see that wisdom in action was a wonder to behold. The professors were amazingly knowledgeable, had been trained to perform the way they did at the greatest centres of learning in the world. But they were so saturated with thoughts and theories that they knew even less about the senses, or the openness of everyday experience, than anyone a fraction of their age.

One late afternoon I was lying quite still, face up, eyes closed, on the bed in the middle of my bare little room. Then something happened—perhaps a proof of inspiration in the ancient world, definitely a sign of insanity in this—which for me has tended to repeat itself at certain turning points or crucial moments. Once, a few years later when I moved to Cambridge, it was the voice of a woman that literally spoke out loud and clear as a bell from my solar plexus telling me "You've just got to go deeply inside your soul." My mind, that bizarre piece of apparatus we all have to call our own, took months to get over its shock at the experience and finally let me put her words into practice.

This time a man's voice started talking from deep inside me. I looked everywhere around the room for the speaker. There was no one.

And the voice said, very distinctly: "You have to trace everything back to its source by returning to where your world began." He told me other things, too—that it would be my job always to stay focused on the West because the real solution to every problem, the only lasting solution, lies right at the heart of the problem.

I got up and, even though it was turning dark, went to find the classics department where ancient Greek and Latin are taught. The place looked deserted. The lights were off. But at the very same moment I walked in, a door opened halfway down the lengthy corridor and a man started stepping out; shook my hand and welcomed me warmly; explained that he was head of the department and promised I'd be free, there, to study whatever I chose.

Most of the work I was drawn to, I did on my own. But for one course I developed a special affection because it felt so precious. That was the class, containing three students including me, on ancient philosophy. Together we decided what we really wanted to focus on—the bits and pieces that still survived from the teachings of the oldest Greek philosophers, the so-called Presocratics.

And then something happened that, for me, was totally out of character. Perhaps because I got carried away the night before, and stayed up far too late with a girlfriend, I missed the final class before the Christmas break.

That same afternoon I caught sight of the other two students talking together outside and, as I came closer, both of them burst into laughter. They teased me, taunted me, mocked me, told me that because I missed the class they'd already taken the best assignments for our vacation essays. And I'd been left with the worst possible subject for mine: the most unrewarding, the obscurest and dullest.

I was going to have to write my essay on someone called Empedocles.

But as I'd already come to discover, the most important choices in life are never made by us. They are always made for us.

I had a sense that this essay was going to be something unusual. And an irresistible instinct told me to get out of Europe: to step away from those dense patternings of thought and invisible forms of culture that prevent us, in spite of our apparent intelligence or insights, from seeing clearly. So I packed a small bag with the ancient Greek text of Empedocles, plus the most authoritative translation of his words into English as well as a dependable Greek dictionary, and hitchhiked down through France and Spain to Morocco.

Sitting by the window in a tiny Tangier hotel, pacing around on the roof, walking through the streets or along the beaches, I started letting Empedocles' poetry slowly filter through me—because that's how he spoke, not as a dull philosopher but as an incantatory poet.

And I became more and more confused.

On the one hand here were Empedocles' own words, powerful images and sounds with the strangest depths of implication and meaning crashing against each other like cresting waves in a storm at sea. On the other hand, here was the Cambridge University Press translation of those same words: completely flat and calm, childishly clear and simple, as rational as rational could be. And there was hardly any correspondence, let alone some real relationship, between the two.

This was no translation. Empedocles in all his wildness had been censored, removed; and something else attributed to him had, by some mistake, been put in his place.

I stayed with Empedocles' words day after day, swaying like a lost boat in a heaving ocean. And I became weaker and weaker.

I stopped being able to eat; a strange pain in the stomach kept getting stronger. Soon I could hardly walk outside or climb the stairs to the roof. Eventually I didn't even have the energy needed to sit on a chair and just lay in bed—until I realized I'd have to take action very quickly.

The next morning I dragged myself out of the room to catch a boat for Spain and, barely conscious, hitchhiked without stopping all the way to England. It was Christmas Day when I arrived at my parents' home in London. They weren't there but I knew where the keys were, went to my room and lost consciousness.

It was a couple of days before they came back, found me in bed and rushed me to hospital. The nurses forcefully brought me round so they could prepare me for surgery: I was suffering from acute appendicitis. Then I went unconscious, again, from the anaesthetic. And instead of going blank, something else happened.

I was taken into Empedocles' world.

Right at the start of his most important teaching he introduces the four elements that were later to become so famous in western science: water and fire, earth and air. And he explains that they are the roots of all existence.

But for him they weren't simple substances stripped of any mystery. Every single one of them was a living riddle; was divine. And when it came time for me to sink deep inside the darkness of myself at the hospital I was introduced to each of them in turn—not as concepts or theories but as realities infinitely more real than I am, as the actual building blocks of which my own body and mind and awareness are composed.

I was given the chance to touch and taste and feel the pulsing divinity of these elements just as Empedocles had described them. I had the direct experience of seeing how the whole of creation grows out of them and that, aside from each of them, nothing else exists.

And there he was—the invisible being who years earlier left his fragrance when he came to visit—showing me his universe, taking care of me, perfectly free to move at will between the pretty world of the senses and the vast spaces hidden inside your body or mine.

In a split second which could also have been an eternity, I realized the shattering truth that this man was the master not only of my conscious life but of my unconscious existence as well. He was there at the beginning, there at the end; inside, outside. And that was that.

And there I stayed with him, quite conscious, just he and I alone together.

11

Opening my eyes in hospital—room, bed, light leaning through the window—was not what I might have expected.

When you've seen the source of people and trees and everything else in between, nothing looks or feels the same again. This was no experience of coming back to reality. It was an awareness, more acute than ever, that I'd left reality behind.

Of course I did my humorous and patriotic best to put it all down to some post-operative hallucination. But hallucinations mostly last for a while, then fade away.

Not only did this stay. For the life of me I couldn't find anything, here, worth doubting or suspecting in comparison with the collective hallucination that makes every shape and image and figure feel real.

And flowing through it all was the uncanny sense, which refused to go away, that what little remained of my life was no longer my own. I was living, whether unconscious or conscious, the poetry of a man who'd been alive over two thousand years ago—and happened to be known as a god, not to mention a magician, in his time.

My world was becoming the universe of Empedocles.

From here on, a compelling logic kept shaping the way events unfolded week after week and day by day. At first it seemed an intensely paradoxical logic, too, but that was because I hadn't yet understood how these things work.

I went back to my parents' home to recover, happy at the thought of being able to return to university and friends and the moors as soon as possible. But I didn't get better: I got worse, much worse. Instead of healing, the wound was so badly infected I ended up almost unable to move for nine months.

And in spite of the weakness, the frustration, the frequent pain and inconvenience, I couldn't help knowing deep inside myself exactly what was happening.

None of this was accidental. Nothing had been a coincidence ever since that fragrant visit all those years ago, or my absence from class on the day essays were assigned, or the journey to Tangier or the sickness.

All that time, Empedocles had been pulling the strings from behind the scenes where he could see me but I could only sense him.

And now he had me exactly where he wanted me— and he wanted me all for himself.

There would be no distractions here, no escape, no forgetting. Every available avenue of ordinary avoidance for a teenager to explore had been neatly, and very effectively, cut off. I belonged to him.

Adjusting to a situation as unusual as this doesn't take a minute, even a month. It takes a lifetime—and that, too, is nowhere remotely close to long enough.

But soon something started shifting inside me and, as well as accepting the inevitable, I found it oddly comical. Later, there was another shift and the only thing I could do was melt; surrender.

Slowly shuffling between my bedroom and the living room downstairs, I realized nothing was left for me aside from devoting myself to his work—and to the fateful essay which had set so much in motion.

I knew something was drastically wrong with the orthodox translations of Empedocles. And I knew something was even more terribly wrong with the standard explanations of his teachings. But I didn't know what was wrong, or how.

Neither did I know where to start. There was something so magically elusive and subtle in Empedocles' poetry that not even the best-trained experts could hope to follow him or keep up without tripping over, falling flat on their face. And I realized I'd just have to start, from where I was, by doing the only thing I could do.

I was going to have to surrender completely to every moment by respecting and attending to each single thought that came along. There was no way I could tell which idea might be sound, no chance of knowing where any thought would be going or whether it was headed in the right direction.

So I wrote them down one by one without exception or the slightest censorship, sitting next to the garden window on the living room sofa, inside a notebook.

The moments of time began steadily aligning closer and closer to each other as if moving towards an invisible point. Everything—the birds, trains shaking in the distance, news, even the pain—became a more insistent reminder of my need to know what Empedocles was really saying, or doing, through his poetry all those centuries ago.

And one spring morning, with my pen about halfway down the left-hand column on the open page, I watched as I wrote a paragraph consisting of one small sentence along a single line that expressed the only thing I cared for: "Please, God, show me the whole truth of Empedocles' teaching."

Almost as soon as I see the words written, it's already over. In a few short seconds at the very most, everything has been given. It's all being shown to me—visually, diagrammatically, in depth, simultaneously. Nothing is left out.

There it is: not in shreds or fragments but the whole of Empedocles' teaching staring through every bit of it, perfectly together and intact without the time or space for even a passing thought to get in the way. As if some seed has suddenly sprouted inside me, I'm able to see the entire moving reality along with each detail of how it works; the secret, crucial pivoting point around which everything revolves; what's been missed by his interpreters, lost, forgotten; what's been misunderstood and mistranslated for millennia, distorted beyond any possible recognition, turned inside out and twisted back to front.

And I saw for myself how naïve it is, how infinitely foolish, to believe that the earliest Greek philosophers were just naïve or primitive fools in contrast to the sophisticated humans we've become. Empedocles was unbelievably devious, a master of trickery who knew he didn't have to trick anyone because people are so desperate to trick themselves.

He was an expert at hiding behind his own words, at making apparently simple comments that would send his brilliant interpreters—now just as much as then— scuttling off in the wrong direction. He always had his finger on the pulse of the unexpected, and the only idiots in this are ourselves.

From that quick sequence of seconds onwards, it was simply a matter of allowing his story to unfold: of letting the timeless roll out into time. And even my life was his story now, no longer mine.

The circle had been closed. In asking that question I made my final request; in being presented with that answer I'd been given everything. But for everything there's always a price—and I would have to give everything in return.

This was a very different world to get used to now, one with rules that aren't the same as in our normal human games: a world where, exactly as in Empedocles' own teaching, everything is the reverse of what any sensible or level-headed person would expect.

Here the loss of one's freedom is the greatest freedom; the perfect act of free will is giving one's free will away and the best choice is to leave all choice behind. Here good can be bad and bad will often be good.

There's nothing nice here. All those illusions about being in charge of our lives, of believing life is meant to serve or fulfil us, about being the central point around which everything revolves, are blown away and gone before there was any chance to see where they went. Here cosy notions are the first item to be destroyed.

Here illness, incapacity, aren't always something to be avoided and healed. They may have to be used or even produced for a particular purpose, becoming an insignificant part of the price we need to pay.

And to give one's life for a question asked, then answered, in a few seconds is not only fair—it's a bargain.

12

THE PRECISION of existence can never be known by the human mind.

That's why the goal of every woman and man is to become human but the purpose of being human is to leave everything human behind. To discover this precision, one has to stop being a human and start being the mystery of life itself.

The first time Empedocles came to me, long before I had any clue who he was, he couldn't be seen. He couldn't be touched. And when eventually I came to read his words recorded thousands of years ago, there he was saying just the same thing—that what's real, divinely real, can't be touched and can't be seen. What he did is what he said; what he'd said is what he did.

These beings, these uncanny unknown creatures, say what they do and do what they say. There is no difference between the two. And I too do the same, right now, in writing this.

Of course from any ordinary perspective that's hard to understand, which is why sooner or later everything ordinary has to be put aside. The rule is that this should always be done gently, though. If people were to see too quickly how deceived they are, the never-living lives they are being expected to live, they'd go crazy or die of the shock.

But that changes nothing—in the same way that nothing changes the fact of what happened during those weeks and months.

Just as I hadn't been alone while unconscious in the hospital, I wasn't alone now. Empedocles was there, waiting in the living room when I came downstairs; or he would suddenly appear at some point in the day.

We would both stay alone together, the two of us in total silence. And I was confronted with the strangest reality I could never have imagined. Here was a teacher who would always stand behind every other teacher: the teacher at the root of oneself.

But neither could anything change the fact that, to get close to what's untouchable and invisible, I would have to become invisible and untouchable myself. Like it or not, there's no other way to spend time with someone who can't be touched or seen. It was the simplest, most obvious matter: like coming together with like.

And this is why, from that time on, I have had no body or legs or arms. The only way to tell this precisely is to say that, even for writing these words right now, I have to borrow a pair of hands.

Sometimes that can almost feel easy. Sometimes, depending on the conditions prevailing at any given time, it's unbelievably hard. There are things to be considered, factors taken into account, after returning to the root of oneself.

Duties don't disappear. On the contrary: they become clearer, starker, far more urgent than before. And they become even more impossible to communicate—of course there are many degrees of impossibility—except in the darkest moments of love. Otherwise, people can't help being fooled into wanting to believe that you're looking at them while the whole time you only have your eyes on the task at hand.

And already, back then, the task was very simple.

Just as I'd written down the question, now I'd have to write out the answer. But it's always such a slow, exacting process. All the words are useless unless they first become fine needles for sewing a certain substance inside the soul.

And when the answer's been written out in full, then I'll be able to go.

LEARNINGS

13

SURRENDER doesn't just happen once, then get tucked away in some corner.

It's wild, incessant: one wave always swallowed by another, then another. It's what makes you truly human because it's so much more than any human can bear.

And this is the way you end up no longer living inside time—by becoming time instead, as each single moment keeps dying to make way for the next.

Life flowed on, although it's no easy matter to help break the sleep of a world that's broken every rhythm of the sacred. The essay grew into a dissertation and eventually was done. But that's neither here nor there when each breath and step taken are another word inside the book you've been asked to write.

Soon the offers of research scholarships were coming in from a range of universities—London, St Andrews, Oxford. And it was an incredibly beautiful woman who, at the end of the day, decided me to accept the invitation that arrived from Cambridge.

But nothing, no one, could have prepared me for the incompetence and utter corruption of the funny little people I encountered there. They honestly seemed to believe they were wise, involved in something important, although they didn't even know how to live their lives or read the texts right in front of their eyes.

Studying them and watching how they worked, talking with them, observing the ways they spoke, I started seeing the full scope of the fictions and fantasies they kept weaving—not only around Empedocles' poetry but around everything they touched. It wasn't their fault, because they are just a small part of the carefully feathered plan to help everyone forget.

I've never met more than two or three scholars, at the very most, who genuinely wanted something real: who would take a lengthy breath before admitting they'd got it wrong all along and were so relieved to be able to see what they'd missed. And they were the absolute best in their field.

At Cambridge, though, the only truth was out in the streets where love could show her face—and where desire, at last, stopped changing shape so she could whisper her secrets in my ear.

The way it happened was like this. For my work on Empedocles I had to do a touch of reading. But more than anything else I needed to meditate deeply, very deeply: be taken into places where nothing exists in any direction except purest space.

That's when the problem appeared, just like some kind of gatekeeper.

Each time I went into meditation and was about to leave everything behind, a craving would come over me for some item of food. There seemed nothing at all I could do. If I dismissed the thought of wanting this or that and ignored the craving, it came right back.

But if I gave in and went to get the food and eat it, then again the craving came straight back.

I was stuck, trapped, helpless. In the past I'd learned if I had a problem to ask for help wherever I could find it. This time, though, I realized I would have to face this impossibility all alone.

With tremendous effort—as if there were forces determined not to let me look—I started sensing the great trick that was being played, not only on me but on everyone alive or dead. And gradually it dawned on me what the secret was.

Even when I went out to eat that food, I never actually ate it myself. And the reason I never ate it is because, at the precise moment of supposedly enjoying the item I'd gone to so much trouble to find, my mind had already moved on.

Those moments of tasting are the most transient, most fragile experiences imaginable—which is a whole mystery in itself. In actual fact they vanish, like birdsong, into another world where the purest essence of all taste and all fragrance is one. But that's a reality we never notice because we are already thinking about something else; then something else.

I realized I was being fooled. And in that moment of realization I also saw what I needed to do. I couldn't ignore my mind. Neither could I fight it. But what I could do is to treat it with absolute seriousness and follow it wherever it led.

One afternoon I was sinking into meditation when, as usual, I was abruptly interrupted by the craving for a special taste—the taste of a particular cheesecake made by a bakery in Cambridge. So I jumped on my girlfriend's old bicycle and rode across town; bought a slice of the cheesecake and went to sit on a bench in the park, determined not to miss a single trick.

As soon as I put the first piece in my mouth, it happened. My mind had completely abandoned the cheesecake and already switched to wanting something else. I had to look hard for a few seconds to understand what it was really after, or seemed to want: a slice of some apricot dessert that I'd eaten once or twice before at a café in London. And the game began.

As quickly as I could, I headed for the main road out of Cambridge and hitchhiked down to London. I went straight to the café—it was getting dark now—and joined the line-up of people waiting to be served.

Ahead of me, I could already see the portions of apricot dessert inside the glass display case. It would only be a minute, maybe two, before I'd have the chance to satisfy the dull craving for the sake of which I came all the way to London: to demonstrate, unmistakably, just how serious I was.

But I never reached the counter. With what it had been asking for on full display, right in front of me, suddenly my mind had jumped again. Before I even had the time to buy a portion, apricot dessert was old news and I was already thinking of something else—of the dark chocolate I'd once glimpsed in the window of a little shop up the hill and around the corner.

Instantly I left the café, walked up the hill, was just about to turn the corner: obedient servant of my desire, faithful slave, dead set on following through to the very end whatever that end might bring.

And before I could turn the corner it was all over.

I stopped by the side of the road as it, he, she revealed itself—sacred source of all desire, the divinely magical origin of every single craving or longing in our minds. We have no idea that, every time we go somewhere in search of something we want, we are walking with the gods.

Desire has a trillion forms, transforms itself into shape after shape; but the tragedy is that we never learn what's needed for coming face to face with desire.

Afterwards I slowly started recognizing what had happened. After all, it's there in the world's myths.

It's there, especially in Homer, with Proteus: revealer of the secrets of nature hidden away since the dawn of time, the god of prophecy who holds all the knowledge of gods as well as humans in his hand. Anyone would be hard put to guess this from his innocent appearance—lying like a seal along the seashore at precisely the point where the water meets land. And if you manage to grab hold of him, he'll keep changing shape from moment to moment a million times; do everything possible, not to mention impossible, to shake you off.

He'll turn into water, change into fire, become any number of animals and people and plants and trees. He'll try any trick to get away.

But if you are able to hold on tight and keep a grip on him, shape after shape, finally he gives up; shares his knowledge; reveals who he truly is.

The divine is what we encounter when, with all our senses open, we genuinely dare to live. Most people laugh at the idea of gods. A few find it thought-inspiring and exotic. Nobody, though, wants the truth: the pedestrian truth.

No one wants to walk with a god.

It wasn't until my last afternoon at Cambridge that I understood to whom I owed such an education. I was sitting outside on my college lawn beside the magnificent chapel, tourists everywhere. Suddenly a graceful woman approached me, in every respect as real as any human; but I knew there was no one else to see her.

She came very close, smiled and thanked me for coming, then introduced herself as the spirit of Cambridge—the divine protector who'd been taking care of the place for ages.

She explained how she is the intelligence of the earth there; how she was the one who drew people to create the university on this specific spot centuries earlier. But for a long time now, nobody has been humble enough to see that all the intelligence expressed through the university really comes from her.

And until humans started to understand, until they stopped dragging her down with their petty claims and fantastically absurd presumptions, she would never be at peace.

Then she smiled again, made the most unusual movement with her head before leaving just as suddenly as she had come.

I learned to take her visit to heart. After all: the sacred isn't some superstition or wishful thinking. It's simply the way things are.

It's the only path that lies ahead when we've left all our superstitions and every dithering thought behind.

Time passed, things changed; people came and went, offered a little or a lot and of course always took a little too.

There were moments of company and comfort, periods of loneliness and freezing: the miracle of being offered an old, cigarette-burned coat one bitter winter even though I would never have thought to ask.

But nothing matters when your heart is focused on what can't be touched or seen. And even the simplest of preparations need preparing for because everything takes forever at the juncture where eternity comes together with time.

Empedocles kept pulling me deeper, drawing me down through the intricate systems of meditation he'd embedded in his poetry—systems of inner cultivation, here at the root of western civilization, which are still so timelessly alive because he knew very well as a magician how to implant them with his life force.

I had to be careful not to mention too much even to close friends, especially to spiritual teachers. The experiences came with such power, were so unhesitatingly direct, that people's faces would turn pale and the old familiar fear would slip into their eyes.

But over the years I found there is nothing more natural than to experience the whole universe inside oneself.

I also found there is nothing more beautiful than to live, again, the meditation practices that once gave rise to our western world—because this world we live in didn't just happen by itself. Long before all the distortions and forgettings it was created out of meditation, because everything without exception that comes into existence has to be fetched from somewhere else.

And in a kind of slow motion I became aware that Empedocles was not alone. There had been others in front of, and beside, and behind him at the dawning of this western world: other great beings who worked together to carry the seeds of a new culture and tend them for the time allowed.

These were the culture–creators and makers and shapers who bring everything into existence from the sacred— logic, science, philosophy, education, medicine, law—only to let people in their arrogance imagine they were the ones who'd done it all. Of course they warn; they remind; they threaten. They'll leave writings as living depositories of their wisdom to guide and teach, although with those who think they're human there can be so little even the guardians of creation are able to do.

But if Empedocles had not been alone, I certainly was: even with friends leaning across the table or ready for another wise, inspiring walk. Then one day I found myself stepping into a North London bookstore during my lunch break from work. I was still wondering why when, quite literally, a book fell on my shoulder and the next moment was lying open at my feet.

As I bent down to pick it up, I was so affected by the words I saw on the page that for a while I could hardly move.

"Know", the words began. Know how "the Greek sages prior to Aristotle" were very great beings who taught that "wisdom can be attained only through a method of spiritual realization; they emphasize the inner effort of spiritual struggle and mystical experience." But, as the text went on, with the passing of time these adepts' teachings would come to be covered over almost completely by all the crowds of imitative intellectuals who imagined they could follow in their footsteps.

I still have that copy of that book. Based on translations from the teachings of Persian mystics, it had been written by a Frenchman called Henry Corbin.

Up until this moment I'd felt like the only person aware that among the earliest Greek philosophers were people who couldn't have been more different, or more distant, from the curious and simple-minded rationalists they are made out in the West to be. They were extraordinarily powerful mystics who had the spiritual methods and meditation techniques needed not only to bring people to reality but to bring entire cultures into being.

Now I was suddenly being shown that others, too, also knew what I knew. And I started to realize what a terrifying joke we've all been learning to live—because the western world has been so negligent of its origins that its own deepest secret had to be preserved for it somewhere else.

While westerners celebrated their inventiveness and cleverness, while they set about destroying everything they touched by playing with the sacred tools they'd been given but had forgotten how to use, there were others patiently taking care of their secret in the East.

And in the West nobody cares because nobody knows. No one even knows the right question, so all the wrong answers keep being given to the questions that were never meant to be asked.

Now, almost the only real questions left are how to bear the pain of living in a world utterly dislocated from its source; how to stay calm when the people preaching calmness are the ones who go on forcing the forgetting even deeper.

And this is the unavoidable price, the ever-present cost, of our neglect: that whatever we wisely do with our enlightened works and finest actions to improve our situation will only make it worse, far worse.

The best of intentions are futile when we've tossed away the key to our reality into the darkness.

ONE NIGHT I saw the most vivid dream.

An extraordinary invitation had come my way. I was being called into some kind of personal library. Lining the shelves, with titles and authors' names very visible, were the exact same books I'd in fact spent years of my waking life longing to turn the pages of and simply be able to read—the rarest of books on mystics, philosophy, alchemy. But because they were so precious, so special, I'd never expected to find even one of them anywhere outside some high-security room in a university.

Then I was told to take all the books I wanted by packing them into as many bags and cases as I could carry. And I was shown that, with them now in my possession, it would be time to be making a big move: to be leaving for somewhere far away.

On waking, I wrote down the dream even though I had no idea what it could mean; tucked it away inside a folder where I found it a quarter of a century later; so totally forgot anything about it that I never for one moment gave it a single thought.

And there are certain things we're not meant to think about. We have our outer lives with their bumps and smoothnesses. Then we have our inner lives with their threads along which we guide and help, are helped and guided—the ties of love, the delicate threads that link and bind us.

But behind our inner lives is the secret that lies hidden even from ourselves: the life that connects us straight to the root of our being.

Several years after this dream I was introduced to the wife of the man who wrote the book that fell on the floor in the shop. He had died but she carried his spirit and the essence of his work like a deep, strong stream.

Soon we became the best of friends and would write, or meet, as often as we could. Each time together brought something new. The moment I would mention some experience I'd had with Empedocles, she would sit bolt upright or rise abruptly to her feet and exclaim in amazement: "But that's exactly what my husband experienced with his teacher!" And as soon as she mentioned details of what happened between her husband's teacher and him, I'd sit straight up or stand abruptly and exclaim: "But that's precisely what happened with Empedocles!"

Little by little, things started becoming clearer.

Henry Corbin's teacher, his *sheikh*, was Suhrawardi: a Persian Sufi from the twelfth century who'd been put to death while still in his thirties for the things he said and did. Suhrawardi claimed he was simply continuing a spiritual lineage which he referred to as the Dawning. But towards the end of what would be such a short life he ran into trouble with orthodox Muslims because he insisted on tracing his lineage a long way back—far beyond even the prophet Muhammad—to the Greeks, and specifically Empedocles.

The reason for him doing this could hardly have been plainer.

Suhrawardi knew he belonged to the same tradition as Empedocles—a tradition not of dead knowledge but of prophetic wisdom which he realized is astonishingly and unstoppably alive, what he described as an eternal leaven which is always bursting unannounced into the world of bodies and time to do its secret work in the ways that it knows best.

And for just the same reason, when Henry Corbin took his wife on a brief visit to Istanbul to examine Suhrawardi's writings but was held there against his will by the outbreak of war, Corbin soon recognized exactly what was happening. He realized without a shadow of doubt that Suhrawardi was holding him there: keeping him all for himself, cut off from every possible distraction, because there was something he needed to do with him undisturbed.

It didn't take long before Corbin found himself immersed inside the process of sitting alone together with the teacher in total silence, even his life no longer his own, being initiated step by step into the lineage of his *sheikh*.

That's how this tradition works; how it reaches out and claims its willing victims. There is nothing conventional or pleasant about it. Whatever tools are available—sickness, war—will be used quite ruthlessly, impersonally, for the task at hand.

That's the hard core of this tradition. And his wife would sometimes talk, with more than a little frustration, about the intellectuals in France who proudly imagined they were continuing her husband's work. Then she'd look at me with a timeless combination of seriousness plus the gentlest smile while saying: "But in what really matters, you are my husband's successor."

During those mornings and afternoons and evenings we spent together, a lot was said. For her part, above all she kept emphasizing her husband's absolute refusal to compromise—even a fraction of a millimetre, let alone an inch—on anything important.

In a world where everyone is bending over backwards, he held fast to his vision; would never flinch.

Then—just as I was preparing to get married and move with my wife from England to the west coast of Canada—I received a message from her inviting me to Paris. And there was one peculiar request in her letter that profoundly puzzled me at the time. She specified that I should bring with me as many empty cases or bags as I'd be able to carry.

When I came, we talked for days. Finally she got up and asked me to follow as she opened the door to her husband's library. She led me in and there were the very same books I'd been shown by my dream: the identical titles and authors lining the walls, just as I'd seen them.

And she said I should take all the books I wanted, the most precious ones, by putting them inside the bags and cases I'd brought with me.

That was the last time I ever met Stella Corbin, although I would send friends to visit her long after my wife and I had left Europe.

But the song of the Sufis, once it starts, never ends.

There is a traditional saying that you should never waste your time trying to find real Sufis because they are the ones who will find you. And this turned out to be perfectly true.

As if out of nowhere, the representatives or heads of different Sufi lineages would suddenly appear at different times to help me in ways no other humans ever could. They would offer their blessing for my work years before I knew what work I had to do. They would lend their support in the subtlest, most selfless of ways. When needed, they would literally save my life.

One of the strangest things is that I'd never call myself a Sufi. But the strangenesses are everywhere in or around this mysterious substance linking me to Empedocles as it threads its way into and out of other traditions while weaving across culture after culture, leaving almost no trace as it touches and transforms those traditions from behind, never staying visible long enough to compromise or be corrupted, endlessly adjusting, moving, adapting, appearing only to disappear as it arrives fresh and renewed from eternity before heading straight back the moment its work is done.

If you happen to glimpse it, it can look like anything else: like a bird at the foot of a tree.

But the next minute it's gone.

And the work allocated to it is more arduous than words could say. This tradition will never be at home in any culture because it's what gives rise to cultures, then helps bring them to a close by doing and saying what's needed. Its job is to make the impossible real and to leave everything possible behind: is to keep breaking a path through the impassable mountains for the sake of creating an opening into the day that's always waiting, although people's faces are all turned the other way.

This, in reality, is how whole worlds are born.

And this is also the way they die—through the kind of unbroken labour that almost no one can bear to see.

DAWNINGS

16

The DAWN of a civilization is infinitely significant.

Something new comes into being that will shape and define the whole of existence for millions of people over hundreds or thousands of years. And these people either remember the impulse that gave rise to it, making its original purpose their own.

Or they forget it—and there's chaos.

Chaos always comes from taking something real, then turning it back to front to suit one's purposes. And, just so we could forget as completely as possible about our forgetfulness, we invented the myth of progress.

As solutions go, it was a clever if desperate move. But all this illusory movement towards some imaginary goal raises more questions than it can ever answer; wounds far more people than it will ever be able to heal.

So everybody curls up to die without the answers that soothe and restore, without the remedies that put our minds at rest.

The concept of progress only has one purpose or aim: to compensate for the essential truth, abandoned and then disposed of long ago, that the dawning of a civilization is something sacred. So people end up looking to other cultures for the sacredness they lost in theirs—try harder, then harder, to scrub away the knowledge buried in their bones.

And they'll do whatever they can to erase any memory of those sacred obligations that, as surely as day follows night, come with participating in a culture.

Now it's more or less impossible to talk about such things. And even if someone wants to listen, somewhere, that doesn't help too much because these obligations will be interpreted straight away as some deeply esoteric or mystical duty.

But there's nothing esoteric or exclusive about them. They are just what's been left to the foolish few who agree to take on the work of humanity which humanity refused to do.

Completely forgotten is the fact that our minds are not for ourselves. Our spirituality, our brilliant moment of inspiration, of alertness or intensity, is not for us. Neither are our lives because we are here to serve the cosmos, not ourselves.

All nature is waiting for us to become conscious because there's a particular quality of consciousness that only humans can provide. Nature needs that consciousness; cries out for it. And the process of deciphering nature's need, then discovering how to respond to it, is what's called learning to become human.

The truth of being a human is this—that the whole of existence has to be maintained from moment to moment, day after day, by the attention of those who are able to do so. Without such constant, conscious attention it would all disintegrate so quickly that nothing would be left but an empty memory of how things once could have been.

People love talking cheerfully about how love makes the world go round. What they don't know is that if they ever managed just to glimpse the reality of love, the power behind each gesture of affection, they would be crushed to death in an instant.

Love, for this tradition, is to cut a route through the dark mountains where no path could have existed before. But once that road has been cleared, thanks to the most back-breaking efforts imaginable, everyone follows happily as if the highway had always been there—putting up different signs and booths and stalls.

This is the secret of how new cultures are created. One day a few people wake up, see so much laid out ready in front of them and wonder what to make of it all. They can't grasp that nothing would exist, that the sun wouldn't rise in the sky, without the help of those who work so lovingly behind the scenes.

Planets don't move by themselves. Even the light of the sun and moon and stars has to keep being refreshed from eternity. But with our selfishness and forgetfulness we don't just kill the animals, destroy the water and earth and sky. We suck the sunlight dry; drain away the livingness from reality itself. And by the time a particular point has been reached, when a certain degree of inhumanity has been touched, then the experiment is already over.

To become human has always meant the same thing.

It's to become the dawn behind the dawn. But dawn can't be understood in our words or in our world—this world that's disintegrating so quickly. The only way to do that is by entering the realm of dawn.

Every single moment is a doorway leading into reality. And the doorway of dawn is thinner than a slit but larger than the whole of creation, because everything comes through it.

In reality the time of dawn is all there is: sweet miracle, gracious, patient everpresence. This is the time of dawn, so dawn is all there is. And now is the time of dawn because dawn is all there is.

All time is the time of dawn. The light of the day is the light of dawn while the light we carry through the night is still the light of the dawn.

And we, ourselves, are nothing more than figments of the dawn reaching out to touch each other—stroking morning's wings.

17

THE BIRDS are so quick to sing the dawn.

Don't think for a minute it's because they have nothing better to be doing with their time. It's just that they are so much closer to reality than those would-be, strange-furred humans who keep chattering to themselves when they're not even saying a word.

We can take you there. But the question is whether you are ready to come.

We are always here, and here and here, ready when no one else is—singing, calling with all due harshness and sweetness to reach you, speaking so openly those secrets that haven't failed to fall on barren soil because not even a handful of you ever took the simple steps needed to learn our speech.

But we never give up easily.

We are the announcers of beginnings and endings, the markers of your time; definers of your possibilities, the full-throated chorus at your grave. While you stay ignorant of what we're saying, you stay ignorant of yourselves. And when you've driven us out, you have chased yourselves away.

Don't make the mistake of taking this for poetry or metaphor or allegory. On the contrary, until you understand it you're not even a poetic metaphor for what a human should be. And in spite of the achievements you love to count off, one by one, your existence is nothing but an allegory of life thrown away.

There was a time in my twenties, like so many others after or before, when I was forced to leave any beaten track: thrown off all those convenient railway lines we almost always follow when we're perfectly sure we must be forging our own path.

It was something mysterious inside that kept calling, ordering me to meditate in a certain way. So, for about three years, each day—and not just each day but every moment of each day—I meditated on the singing of the birds.

For all those days and years it never once occurred to me to analyze the sounds. I never named them and said that's a blackbird, a robin, a crow. Instead, I was constantly present for every bird call: waiting for it before it sounded, ready to wrap it in awareness, closely attentive to whether it came from nearby or far away.

Just as most people are only interested in the sound made by other people talking, I was only interested in whatever the birds had to say.

Then in the night when they'd gone to sleep, my meditation was nothing else but waiting patiently until they'd wake up and start singing again. Even when there wasn't a chirp, all I cared for or had ears for—hour after hour—was the absence of their song.

This went on and it went on. I never questioned its purpose, or doubted. And the conversation of the birds filled my life month by month, year after year.

But one day it happened—just like a bird taking off or landing on a lake.

Everything was the same as before, except that nothing whatsoever was left apart from their singing. And I was understanding the language of the birds as effortlessly, as completely, as I used to understand English.

I was in their world. I felt and knew their sky, which isn't our sky. I saw their earth, which is infinitely more real and detailed and coloured than ours. And you may find this too nonsensical, just too absurd; but somehow and somewhere you know.

Everything speaks. Communication is everywhere— because the fact of existing is the act of communicating. In me, instantly accessible at any moment, was all the wisdom of the birds that had ever lived because I could speak and hear and understand their speech.

Eventually my body could walk again; look and move like a two-legged, two-armed man; talk with other people, work. There was no division between here and there, no contradiction or disharmony. On the contrary: until you experience what it actually means to be taken into another world you can never realize the full purpose of living in this.

In fact it's only when you are able to see things from the point of view of nature, not just from the peopled point of view, that you can set out on the path of being human. And then you become really grounded, far more grounded than the biggest cynic or sceptic.

But in this back-to-front world which only offers fake impersonations of a human being, I seemed to become less and less human. It's as if I was some peculiar creature perched on the edge of being a man—even though some deeper nature would inevitably show through.

When I started accepting invitations to give talks and managed to open my mouth, I'd speak as a bird. I would call to those who could hear: sometimes predatory or sometimes sweet. But the silences between the bursts of song were always as important as any sound.

And when I wrote, it was to put on paper what the birds are doing. They are singing not just to their mates, not just for the crops or the sun but for you—calling you to break out of your husks and sprout from the seeds you were sown as, begging you at last to grow up.

We are guardians and protectors, watchers, peacekeepers, educators, jury and judge. Every movement of ours is an announcement; each call you're empty enough to hear is an oracle.

And the fact that different kinds of birds have different songs is the foundation of all the divine mysteries.

This is why ancient traditions spoke about the language of the birds and were so quick to connect deciphering it with the skills of prophecy. Later, but too late, prophets tried laying down firm rules for divination based on the sounds made by birds and the ways birds flew—because they were already forgetting.

Now there's hardly a feather left. No reasonable person would even want to touch on the subject. And those who are supposed to be wiser will gladly insist that what used to be called the language of birds of course doesn't refer to actual birds: it's just some fanciful metaphor for the ethereal language of angels.

The simple fact is, though, that it's only the presence of birds in this world—their physical, shitting selves—which makes them messengers from that. And when the messages are no longer heard, then our whole world falls apart.

But don't think I am saying anything at all aside from the sound of my words, because I'm just calling directly from reality.

It's quite true that birds sometimes bring messages about the future: come to warn, offer prophecies. Even so, that's only the smallest part of their job.

Their main aim has always been what it still is—to draw us away entirely from ourselves. And to be taken into their world is instantly to be shown the truth of our almost human reality.

It's to understand why this virtual existence is still nowhere close to becoming human. It's to notice how far we drifted away from life and never came near to being real.

Listen well and it's to hear the whole story of our world: where it came from, what it will be, how it was, the way it is.

And only then this bird stops calling; and the song ends just where it began, because its last note will be its first.

18

I<small>T'S ONLY RIGHT</small> to say a little, this one last time, about the bringers.

They are the hopeless ones who know they can do nothing. They know they can't create anything real. They know they can't help anyone at all.

They know they can't change a single thing for the better. They know they can't say anything right.

So they throw themselves away into the darkness they came from; leave all the lights and clarities of existence far behind like the street lights of a tiny village on a long, long night's road; sink deep into the underworld and disappear.

There, in the depths of darkness, it's always the same. Whatever could be useful or needed is put into their hand at the last moment with perfect care so that when they come back they'll be able to help and create, say and do.

This isn't death. It's death upon death because it starts well before physical death, then never ends. And eventually, paradoxically, even the body becomes accustomed to it— although there's no getting used to the uselessness of doing anything else without this.

The rules are simple. Prepare in silence. Train in stillness. Strain as much as possible to become worthy of facing the impossible. Maybe you'll be unlucky, or lucky, enough to be chosen but the chances are you won't. It's much more likely someone else will be picked who is far simpler and purer than you, untrained, unprepared: the timeliest reminder of what matters most.

Intelligence, everything anyone would think of as intelligence, is entirely irrelevant. It's just a question of being empty enough to transmit the will and wisdom of the gods.

And out from the darkest depths come the bringers of light and rightness, of justice and laws, with both feet planted in the night but the gift of dawn in their hand.

Sometimes they bring laws for their city or state or country. And sometimes they'll come with the laws for a whole culture: Parmenides, who was particularly close to Empedocles, is a good example.

Right at the start of the poem he wrote two and a half thousand years ago, he describes being brought by daughters of the sun onto the path kept open for the sun itself through the darkness every night. It's just the same path now, as then, as ever.

You go to that place where the sun sets—then rises inside you.

Down there in the depths he meets the queen of death: so happy to see him, so welcoming, so friendly. And she hands him something, tells him to take it away. But that something is not exactly what's to be expected from a goddess at home in another world.

The gift she gave him is the laws of logic. And this is why Parmenides has stayed so famous, right down to today, as the father of reason and rationality.

But there's just one, tiny fact that always gets left aside because everything else depends on forgetting it.

Logic was never designed to trap people into thinking they could think intelligently and rationally about this, or that. Instead, it was intended to tear every bit of reasonableness to shreds and leave them in a ditch at the side of the road—because the logic brought by Parmenides didn't come from him.

It was a gift from the gods, specially created to take whoever's ready straight back to the gods. Fetched out of the depths, it was meant to carry humans all the way to the place it had arrived from: to a stillness where nothing in you moves for thousands of years, where you become the source of everything you perceive, and you learn to bring both worlds together as the living face of death.

Just like the poetry left by Empedocles, Parmenides' words don't refer to some reality. They don't talk about what's real. They are that reality themselves, still dripping with the divinity they came from.

The particular way they move from another world into this, their moment of contact and entry: nothing could be easier to demonstrate. But it can only be experienced when you've discovered how to throw yourself away.

And he made sure, like other lawbringers, to pass on the warning call he'd already heard himself. It's the cry that says: Don't ever forget these primordial laws. Don't for a moment think of changing them. Don't even dream of adding anything else. Don't be a fool and take anything away, leave anything out.

Don't mess about; don't play around. Don't interfere with the intricately subtle process of nature and try to alter its pace or course. These words will grow in their own good time according to the laws inside them—if only they are left alone.

To see how well that worked out, one just has to look at the devastation all around.

In their fear of what's always waiting over the horizon, people will try anything to hold on to some lingering sense of self-importance. They would never allow for a moment that the achievements they are so proud of issue from the slow smile of a goddess.

And rather than letting their little rationalities be torn apart, they started tearing Parmenides' teaching to shreds instead: destroyed every bit of sense in it they could find.

Everything he'd worked so hard to say was shifted, twisted, misplaced. As for the discoveries, made years ago in his own hometown, about who he had really been: they were shuffled away out of sight. Philosophers fell over themselves to dismiss the evidence that the founder of western logic was an expert at entering other states of consciousness, a master of ecstasy and incantation, a prophet no less than Empedocles, a healer, interpreter of dreams; that he belonged to a line of priests responsible for going into the darkness and bringing whatever's needed for us here out from the world of the sacred.

The truth is that our entire existence and everything in it, including logic, comes from the sacred. Without that sacred source there are no real words to be spoken, no voice to say them. And when the laws needed for living are all invented by people, when instead of being fetched from another world they're just fetched from another room, there is already no explaining how lost we are.

But for anything to come from there to here, from that world into this, the path has to be kept clear: quite open. And for it to stay open there have to be those who are willing to go where others won't—who are prepared to keep the road well travelled as far as Persephone, the queen of death.

It's simply a matter of going to meet death before death comes looking for you.

As long as there are those empty enough to do this, the sun is still able to shine. They are the ones who come carrying the nourishment for every culture, who even bring the air that's needed to breathe—because there is nothing as fresh as what's been fetched straight out of the darkness, nothing as alive as what's just arrived from the world of the dead.

So when the rest is all forgotten, remember: there's not one single thing more precious than this.

And nothing could be more fated than a culture that throws those gifts away.

THREE

BREAKING

19

I HAVE SAID all that I had to say; already done everything needed.

But sometimes once is not quite enough. And now I have to cover the same ground again almost from the start—this time facing the other way.

Unvisited, no one ever survives very long. In fact our lives are silently shaped, even defined, by the various gifts our visitors bring. And while some guests come in through the front door, others tend to follow a different route.

The fragrant guest wasn't my only visitor when I was still around ten or eleven. Those were days of formal as well as informal introductions—although it couldn't have been easier, even then, to sense where things would all be ending up.

Behind the house where I lived as a child was the garden. And behind the garden was the darkness.

As an area it seemed small enough, from outside. But it became surprisingly large when one wandered in. Tall, unchecked trees kept out the sunlight and it was a place where nobody had the slightest reason to go.

Funnily enough, truth always comes from those places where no one has any good reason to go.

One day I had a vision in the form of a visit; a visit in the form of a vision. It was something impossible to describe with ease to anyone: so familiar and so unexpected, so unforgettably strange. But of course everybody knows in private those areas better unmentioned, best left alone.

And yes, it was all in my imagination—just as this whole world is the little fiction inside yours.

I saw myself out in the garden beside our home. A man, weighed down with old age, was slowly but steadily making his way into the other end of the garden from the unknown area beyond. There was no life left in him, only the energy needed to take a few hard breaths as he walked towards me with all the seriousness and dignity he could find.

When he'd come to a stop and we were standing together, me facing him and him in front of me, the scene was as vivid as if I was looking straight at both figures through brand new glass.

And as though the act of giving would be the last thing he'd ever be able to perform, he handed me a document like an official piece of paper which he had been carrying all along.

I could see every detail of the precise handwriting crystal clear. Near the top of the page was the title, followed by a simple poem. But I didn't have to read a word because the old man was reciting everything out loud:

Child

my words are broken

by the birds that thread their

music through my days

scattering all I have

to say as if it had

no worth

And as soon as the words left his mouth, they were broken and swept away by the breeze and a blackbird here or there or here.

They were a summary of his life, his entire existence, the fullest wisdom he could muster. The poem's title said it all. But there was no way they'd escape the fate that the poem itself was describing. Even they were scattered and swallowed by the sounds of life the same second they'd been spoken.

Just the reading of them was their dissolution and destruction. And this was the old man's legacy—nothing but a testament to utter emptiness.

As for myself, I was young enough; not yet a teenager. But I realized instantly, without the smallest room for hesitation or doubt, what the encounter had been intended to convey.

It wasn't a personal message simply being directed at me. Instead, it was a perfect enacting of the fact that all the accumulated smartness of a whole culture—the pretend wisdom of grown-ups who never get even close to grasping what wisdom means—had come to absolutely nothing.

I'd known and seen this already for years. But here it was now, confirmed and sealed and delivered. The only difference between this particular messenger and everyone else was that he saw and knew: stayed humble enough to acknowledge the grand sham nobody has the courage to admit because there's not the slightest good reason to admit it.

Visitors come, visitors go. But here was another guest who would never leave—the feeblest of old men, sounding the heavy beat of death with his feet along with the end for everything.

He became my constant reminder of what's what; wouldn't stop showing me the utter fakery of whatever humans have created unless the breath of the sacred blew it into existence and it sings, true as a bird, straight back to nature.

He showed me how wisdom doesn't come from building clever structures or thinking things up. It comes from being ground down, because the only way to get to the truth is to let yourself be cracked open so that the truth can get to you.

And human wisdom is the joke of jokes: the most exquisite contradiction in terms, the finest fragments of brokenness.

With his recital my life, in any recognizable sense or form, was already over. Every trace of hope or initiative or ambition had been incinerated during the few minutes of that visit to the garden, in a way almost impossible to explain or convey.

So all I'm able to do is what I slowly started learning back then—which is to speak in a different way.

20

THAT OLD MAN'S words spell out the complete pointlessness of all human talking, all human thinking, human living.

This is not the whole story, though—it never is. For anyone strong enough to get over the shock, they also point with the finest accuracy to the reality beyond what's human.

He seems such an ordinary, humdrum visitor. But each single aspect of him, his words, his arriving, is sheer magic. Even by addressing me as "child" he was doing, as I'd only discover years later, exactly what ancient mystics and magicians used to do when in some private place they'd begin transmitting to someone the secrets they knew.

He looked so weak—stripped down to the barest bones of humanity by that same weakness you, too, know perfectly well behind your dumb bravado.

But he had just come out from the back of the garden: a place far too different, too dark, for humans to go. And it was from there, where humans don't dare venture, that he brought the secret of humanity humans themselves don't care to know.

This is the terrible irony of living inside a world which forgot itself and killed off its wise ones, its elders, long ago: that the only way to hear the truth about being human is not from humans but from somewhere else.

It's the predictable result of belonging to a culture where people no longer grow old and wise even when they seem to. They just grow old—a whole spread of cheap tricks stuck up their sleeve as they fill themselves to the gills like crazed creatures with their stimulating hopes and plans, fascinating hobbies and pursuits, good deeds, better thoughts, fancy readings, exotic practices, meditation and travel, getting nice and close to nature while never coming near to growing up.

And the birds have no interest whatsoever in our thoughts. In spite of the hundred wonderful justifications we have for running from ourselves, they don't have a shred of respect for our schemes and dreams.

On the contrary: they are trying all the time to call but we don't hear, to break us away from our nonsense as best they can.

And in the endless circlings of our silliness we are not just wasting the life we've so generously been given. From any bird's-eye view we are a stain on humanity and a betrayal of our reality, because the destiny of humans is not to escape from themselves.

It's to stand firm and face one's brokenness.

But each last intelligent one of us fights our whole life to silence the broken old woman or man inside us. Those who fail become the so-called refuse of humanity: criminals, addicts, the destitute, the lost.

Those who appear to succeed all play their own peculiar games—even turning into wise philosophers, refined psychologists, magnificent visionaries. And they become the real refuse of humanity because they think they can trick fate by refusing to pay their dues; by failing to hand over the price of admission for becoming human.

But if you could only see for just a moment how bad things are, you wouldn't wait for your words to be broken.

You'd go straight ahead and break each one yourself until the pain of the brokenness pulls you right out of human thought and speech altogether—away from your mouth and throat down into the deepest gut where, beyond friendship, beyond discussion, beyond consolation, the ache of longing for the reality of what's sacred is so strong all you can do is shriek and cry from your belly just like the birds.

Then you'll know why the prophets cry and shriek and howl: why, as guardians of the whole of creation, they are always breaking people's words just like birds and scattering everything they say.

For them there are none of those silly ideas about closeness to reality bringing nothing but tranquillity and bliss. On the contrary, as Empedocles already hinted and as Sufis have known only too well, that reality can be far too terrible even to come near.

The nearer anybody comes, the more unbearable the pain—until even physically you feel you are being broken into pieces, smashed to smithereens. And if you happened to have one single ounce of sense still left inside you, you'd be begging for the closeness to be taken away.

That's the reason why true prophets are always mocked and hounded. It's not because they are old-fashioned. They already have been feared and dismissed as crazy for thousands of years.

It isn't because they are dogmatic. In fact they are the least dogmatic people of all—undermining, dissolving, destroying everyone else's dogmas.

The real reason is exactly the opposite: because they restore us to our brokenness.

And, if you can bend down low enough, you'll be able to touch the thread of life that's protected by the prophets; run your finger along the thread once used to hold this world together; feel the texture of the thread weaving through this book.

Then, even when you come back to using human speech and human statements and human stories, you're not really speaking human language at all.

You simply seem to as you wrap and dress a few familiar-sounding words around the language of the birds.

We ALL have that sanctuary of brokenness hidden deep inside us.

It's the place Christ used to talk of. But our overwhelming need for some other, grander kind of home makes us snatch and grab at anything else we think we can grasp hold of and actually imagine we know just what we want.

Nowadays, among most spiritually-minded people, it's the craving for self-realization: the complete freedom of being everywhere and in everything, total liberation even from the limitations of experience, the realization that whatever exists is utter nothingness.

And there's something so devastatingly decisive about the reality of self-realization that those who find it, or allow themselves to be found by it, are almost bound to claim it's the ultimate—to insist it's the final perfection.

It's so different from everything, such a wonderful step outside the collective nightmare of unconsciousness, so astoundingly timeless and new, that whoever reaches there can't help being convinced it's the end.

But it's nothing near. In fact it's just one more shock along the way towards becoming human.

As the ancient Gnostics patiently explained almost two thousand years ago, there is no greater trap than to believe one has arrived at "the completion of all completions"—when in reality one hasn't even arrived yet at the very first mystery of existence behind which all the other mysteries after mysteries lie.

Then even liberation traps us in its net, thanks to the elegance and grace and speed with which we are caught by what we're sure has set us free.

There used to be a time when, twenty four hours a day, I was the Buddha: an unbroken presence, endlessly uninterrupted, just as real while I was asleep as when I was awake.

There was no Buddhism, no Buddhist, no scripture or text—although once I did deliberately visit a Buddhist temple with a huge statue just to meet myself—but simply the reality of the Buddha.

It was a state, if one can call it a state, of unwavering awareness that nothing at all exists except for the purest nothingness: a nothingness which isn't nothing as opposed to something, because it contains absolutely everything together with an absolute compassion for everything that's not yet aware of being nothing.

It was the constant consciousness that there is no face to anything, or anyone, aside from utter facelessness. And there is no access, or path, to that facelessness apart from total pathlessness.

No one ever enters. No one leaves. No path comes in, no path passes through, no path goes out. It remains eternally virgin, perfectly pristine—although people who somehow arrive here will try to place their stamp on it, turn it into a concept or teaching, make it into something.

And it's infinite relief; the end of all searching, finding, seeking, longing, every struggle and effort.

My mind hardly ever moved, night or day, unless I had some problem to solve or a place to go. But I remember once reflecting on my state and noting to myself: So much for all that nonsense about some personal God!

And one June afternoon in 1979—I was halfway through my twenties at the time—I walked into a north London park. Everything started as could be expected, except there was no one there to do any expecting. The nothingness was everywhere in the grass, earth, trees, the squirrels and path, but especially present in the space between objects as well as above them.

Each moment that passed was a movement even deeper inside it, because time is the space of nothingness.

I was sitting on a bench facing a gentle hill of grass bordered, at the far end, by some tall trees when the unexpected happened. The formless nothingness pervading everything started collecting itself and moving—like storm clouds gathering or a bird getting ready to swoop—towards a single point ahead of me, in the sky just above the tops of the trees.

The power behind the movement was so intense it forced me to shut my eyes as I suddenly felt an immense, magisterial energy pressing down on the top of my head and against my ears: pure concentrated emptiness seeping into my brain, working its way through the cells of my body, taking them over, transforming them, moulding them, making them its own.

And as this was happening, the energy had a voice which for some reason I didn't want to hear because it kept repeating: "This is the Descent of the Dove."

I made my way back to where I was living; went into the kitchen; opened the door leading out to the garden; began preparing something to eat. But while I was chopping vegetables, at one particular point my hands slowed down. Then my fingers stopped moving.

I almost knew, before looking up, what I was going to see.

In the kitchen, in the open doorway, extending out into the garden and between the neighbouring houses and beyond—but above all inside the kitchen and filling the doorway—was sheer Presence, sheer power in the Presence, sheer intelligence inside that power. Hovering everywhere and filling the air was the Presence of space, Presence in space, Presence hanging in space, Presence bearing down on space.

I was seeing God face to face. With just the slightest flick he could crush and break me, squash me like an ant and not even notice. For someone who only a little while ago had been laughing at the notion of a personal god, here was the god of Abraham and Isaac: the same as always.

Fear and trembling together with purest terror and awe—that's all that's left when confronted with the omniscient, the all-intelligent, the omnipresent, the almighty, the power and the glory.

There is no end to this story because, behind the curtain of everything we are so certain is real, there is more; then more. And through all the events that would go on unfolding during the weeks to come, in the background there was one thing that kept annoying me: the voice with its words about the descent of the dove.

To begin with, what bothered me was the comparison with Christ—although that soon started falling naturally into place as I came, bit by bit, to adjust to the reality of seeing the Christ as my son.

But it was the fundamental conflict between what I'd just experienced and the biblical accounts of Jesus' baptism that troubled me much more. According to the collective authority and wisdom of the New Testament it was the Holy Spirit, third member of the Trinity, that descended on Jesus like a dove or in the form of a dove.

In my own case, though, I knew without the slightest doubt that what had descended wasn't any Holy Spirit or Ghost: it was God the Father.

I simply accepted living with the strange discrepancy until one day, a few weeks later, I felt a sudden pull to visit the British Museum. But just as I was about to arrive at the entrance I abruptly turned in the other direction, walked down Museum Street until I came to a store called the Museum Bookshop which I had never been in before, went straight in, crossed the floor to a tall bookcase, looked up and brought down a book without even paying attention to its name, then opened the book at random.

It fell straight open for me at the first page of the main text, and my eye was instantly drawn to a statement right in the middle of the very first paragraph. Jesus had returned from the dead to teach his disciples what they didn't know and weren't able to grasp, which is that the first of all the great mysteries encountered by anyone approaching reality—although it's the very last of the mysteries counting outward from reality itself—is the mystery of "the Father in the form of a dove".

Gradually the significance of that sentence in the first paragraph on the first page of this huge Gnostic text, called *Pistis Sophia*, began sinking in; and I realized what had happened.

People nowadays tend to talk about ancient Gnostics without having a clue who they were. For thousands of years Gnostic tradition has been persecuted as a terrible heretical deviation from Christian orthodoxy. But orthodox Christianity with all its beliefs and codes and creeds is the heresy—and the supposedly heretical Gnostics with their direct knowledge of who the Christ was, of what he is, were the original orthodox Christians.

With their inner gnosis or knowing they were part of a tradition weaving through every outer tradition and stretching straight back, in the West, to ancient Greek mystics such as Empedocles. But with the arrival of all the priests and bishops and popes who get attracted to anything real like flies, soon the official Gospels were carefully being manufactured to cover over the original knowing of the Gnostics.

And Christianity, as we know it, became an elaborate curtain drawn over the Christ in the same way that Buddhists—cluttering the nothingness by filling our world with their words and thoughts about emptiness—have drawn their curtains over the Buddha.

We still have a few old Gnostic texts that describe the appalling mess created by so-called Christians with their fancy distinctions between Holy Spirit and Father and Son: that explain how the moment you start throwing words around without knowing what they mean you've completely deceived yourself, not to mention everyone else.

And in their day and age these Gnostics were trying to convey exactly the same warnings Empedocles had already given hundred of years before—that words are the key to understanding the secret of our existence. But when we use them the wrong way as we always do, we are hopelessly deceiving ourselves along with everyone else.

The truth is that to get beyond the fakery of our own words we have to be taken into another world. I was taken there by Empedocles who then introduced me to the other great beings he walks with, because the splintering of reality into Christians and Buddhists and pagans is simply the work of priests and disciples trapped in the trickery of their words.

This is why I have many dear friends who are spiritual teachers from different traditions. But it's also why, despite their apparent equanimity, some are scared to death of sitting with me as I balance their teaching in the palm of my hand.

I roll it around and hold it up to the light of eternity—so bird-like, always breaking people's words.

DYING

22

Times come, for us all, that pose a grave danger to our soul and sanity.

The trouble is that the danger almost always disguises itself as safety—while the real way to safety lies straight through the thick of danger. In other words: it's we who with our quick and careless judgements pose the greatest danger to ourselves.

During my thirties I arrived at a well-reasoned decision which would have been the only major choice I'd ever make for the sake of finding security, comfort, prestige. But, even then, I had the presence of mind to set myself one inner condition.

This was that, before starting out on my new life, I would visit Turkey. Somewhere, I knew, the Turkey that nearly destroyed me as a teenager wasn't done with me yet.

I laid out a summer for the journey—sensing that this was a summer which somehow would begin but never end. The practical details were easy. A contact at Cambridge

University gave me the address for the French Archaeological Institute in Istanbul, together with an introduction to the institute's director, saying I'd be treated there like a king. When I pointed out that I wasn't an archaeologist, he assured me I shouldn't worry because no one would ever know.

Soon after I arrived, the director summoned me to announce he was about to drive across to the other side of the Bosphorus on an archaeological field trip. Very firmly, he insisted I come. The next morning I got up early, feeling heavy, fully aware I was about to be found out.

Eventually he, I, his assistant arrived by jeep at the foot of a big round hill littered with graves all covered in Arabic inscriptions. Endless gravestones for the dead: I couldn't have imagined a less auspicious beginning to my journey.

The only protection I could see from the blazing sun was a pocket of trees, so that was where I went—to sit in the shade throughout the morning and sulk.

After a long wait I heard some shouting: it was time to go for lunch. We drove to a restaurant out in the country that served a choice of meat or meat; and as a vegetarian at the time, my misery was complete. The very French director of the institute was physically, not to mention energetically, enormous. Like a character right out of the world of Asterix he piled into plate after plate of food.

And suddenly, as I was chewing on a shred of lettuce leaf, he threw the inevitable question across at me: "So what's your real purpose here?"

Consciously I didn't have a clue what to say. But, just as suddenly, I heard the words coming up through my throat. "I've come to make contact with Sufis who kept the traditions of ancient Greek mystics and Gnostics alive."

Then he mumbled a comment, between mouthfuls of meat and beer, that I dismissed straight away because I assumed he was playing the usual academics' game of saying something just for the sake of saying it: "Come to my office when we get back so I can help you."

And by the way, he casually added, you may want to know that all the gravestones I've been working on are gravestones for Sufis. Each of them was a dervish. When we get back, climb to the top of the hill and have a look.

I did. Perched on the hilltop was what looked like a complex of ancient ruins. Hidden by a crumbling old wall were an elderly couple sitting beside each other. They gave me a warm welcome and gestured for me to go in.

And inside was a sight I could hardly believe. The inner space was shrouded in soft shade but full of light. Perfectly proportioned, it had twelve equal sides; twelve windows.

The pillar, exactly in the middle, is where I sat. I am not inclined by nature to hallucinations, but the place was completely empty aside from me—and totally alive, streaming with life.

Anyone who had ever been there was still there, doing what had been done for centuries. Nothing in the broken-down hall is absent, nothing lost. Everyone along with everything is going round and round in an intricate dance. But nothing is going anywhere because one is already there.

In the strangest and most unaccountable detail, every aspect of the teachings these Sufis had received—the significance of their symbols and gestures, the meaning behind each movement—was revealed in steps so natural and gentle one didn't even recognize them as steps. Years later I met someone who was an expert in Sufi gathering places and happened to be familiar with that particular spot: a centre or *tekke* for Bektashi Sufis. And, surprised when I described my visit, he said each single aspect of what I'd been shown was historically accurate.

But much more accurate was what I saw about how utterly blind I'd been.

Just beyond where I felt so convinced I was wasting my time is no time at all.

Where I was seeing nothing aside from death, there is nothing but life. Where any of us is, is exactly where we need to be.

And where I feel lost: that's sacred ground.

23

As we drove back into Istanbul, I supposed I'd be back on my own.

But as soon as I offered a grateful goodbye and was stepping away from the jeep, the director of the institute called after me: You're forgetting something.

So, together, we went into his office. And the first thing he did was to explain how his predecessor there during the great war—working away alone on the manuscripts of Suhrawardi—had been Henry Corbin.

He sat me down in the middle of the chaos as people rushed around from desk to desk. Suddenly his secretary, who was sitting right behind me, tapped me on the back so she could hand me a phone.

I put it to my ear and a man speaking French with a deep calm voice told me he'd heard I want to meet him, then invited me to come tomorrow afternoon. We made arrangements and, as I handed back the phone, I asked who it was.

Oh, she said: He's the noblest of the Sufis. And I had the physical sense not of looking ahead, or contemplating my next step forward, but of falling backwards and being pulled straight through a doorway behind me by a force I couldn't see.

Çelaleddin Çelebi was spiritual head of the Mevlevis: successor and living representative, as well as direct descendant in the twenty-first generation, of the most famous Sufi *sheikh* and poet and scholar and madman called Rumi.

There was an indescribably subtle majesty to him— which he clearly had learned, from long experience in different countries, how to hide away. When we met inside his high-walled apartment, the first thing he said was that for years he had the habit of never picking up the phone himself.

But yesterday, as soon as he heard the ring, he became aware he simply had to.

He wanted to know about me; asked what I do. I said I was a writer. And when he asked what I write, I answered that I hadn't yet put anything on paper because I'd been shown there was a book I had to write inside my heart before being ready to produce any outer books.

He gave me a special look and quietly said a couple of words, half to himself, about the Quran.

We didn't stay alone for long. His son-in-law joined us, revelling in the excellence of his British education at the same time as proclaiming his allegiance to Islam.

An exquisite cake was brought in and Çelebi made a point of explaining that a very dear disciple had the cherries regularly flown across and delivered to him fresh from Lebanon.

He tried to say a few things but, instead, let himself be interrupted by his son-in-law—sinking more and more into silence as the steady pressure of educated accusations started building.

"Who on earth do you think you are, coming here to waste my venerable father-in-law's precious time? You are not a Muslim, don't even want to convert to Islam. But Islam is the root and Sufism is the flower. You are pointlessly wasting everybody's time, including yours, by visiting here."

In spite of the provocations, I knew I was simply a guest and sensed how not to react or behave. Politely I sipped my tea as the utter hopelessness of the situation became more, then more, obvious. I'd done my best: had made a sincere gesture in coming. But I wasn't dependent on anyone or anything and had arrived at the point, inside me, where I was ready to break my own expectations by preparing to leave.

Soon the charade, together with the sense of total futility, had reached its climax. I'd had enough. As discreetly as I could, I started inching towards my feet; turned towards Çelebi to thank him for his gracefulness in meeting me. But there was one thing that nothing and nobody would stop me from saying.

"You and your family belong to Islam whereas I don't. Even so, to me the whole essence of Islam is the saying of the prophet Muhammad that we must learn to die before we die. And that is all I care for."

Inwardly, I already had left. But before I could stand fully upright, Çelebi called out: "Stop. Please sit down. Stay with me."

Immediately, everything in the room had changed. The son-in-law, mouth hanging open, became fidgety and restless. And Çelebi came alive.

We stayed together for about three hours in unbroken conversation. But this was no conversation like anything I'd ever experienced before, or would ever experience afterwards.

It was bliss and ecstasy, although that was just at the start. There was no teacher, no student, no first or second. There weren't even two people. Instead, it was the opened flow of something infinite speaking through us to itself.

It needed the whole of you at every moment, completely stripped and transparent, nothing held back. We danced together through a boundless cosmos of purest love and clarity where I knew at each step and in every single instant, without the slightest self-consciousness, with total spontaneity, precisely what to say in response to what he just said: two throats, two mouths, one voice.

And much later I realized this was exactly the same space of sacred communion in which, centuries earlier,

Rumi used to dance with his friend and companion Shams of Tabriz—a space no one else could come into, nobody could share, and that made Rumi's disciples so jealous they eventually were driven to kill Shams off and hide his body.

At one point, during the hours with Çelaleddin Çelebi, he had to excuse himself to go to the toilet. The instant he left the room, the life and strength started flooding back into his son-in-law. In sheer desperation, with as much coherence as he could muster, he started shouting at me: "Who do you think you are, coming here where you don't belong? You don't understand what sacrilege you are committing. Sufism is the room but Islam is the doorway—and without being a Muslim you have absolutely no right to come in!"

Suddenly there was a roar. Çelebi was standing like a lion in the doorway at the far end of the room. "No", he cried. "Leave him alone! You don't understand. He has inside him the holy Quran. The book he is writing inside himself: that is the inner Quran."

And we immersed ourselves again in the flow.

At the end, it was sheer physical exhaustion that forced us to stop. In spite of his age, he wouldn't stop a moment earlier because this was his love and his work and his joy.

Before I left, Çelebi wanted to come back to my writing—the writing that I hadn't even started in any physical sense because I hadn't been shown anything about the shape it one day might take. And he strangely gave his blessing to the work of which I had no conscious knowledge: that I hadn't yet begun.

He also asked me to tell him where I proposed travelling to in Turkey. I said I would probably stop at Konya, Rumi's famous home in the middle of the country; but that my real aim was to get to my own spiritual home of Antakya in the east and then, across the Euphrates, to Urfa which had been the home of one ancient Gnostic very dear to me.

He listened carefully and wrote down two names for me—at the same time providing the necessary guidance and explanations. The first changed my life. The second saved it.

Ever since then, it's been strange to know that I literally owe my life and breath to a Sufi: child of Rumi.

24

S A D L Y we've forgotten the power of paradox to tear our insides out.

Konya is a Mecca for spiritual pilgrims, not to mention tourists; home of the Whirling Dervishes who owe their origin to Rumi; a city steeped in the presence and the memories of Sufis.

But Çelaleddin Çelebi shocked me with the directness of his hidden majesty when he said to me, just before I left:

Don't bother going to Konya with any idea of meeting anybody because no one there can speak like this.

There are the beautiful dances and sayings. There are those who claim to know this or that, who insist they are authorized to teach by me or anyone else.

And then there is this.

But if you do happen to make your way to Konya, he added, make sure to go to Rumi's tomb and only listen to him—because we travel back and forward through the centuries in the blink of an eye.

The utter terror of the paradox didn't start dawning on me until years later when I found myself meeting and sitting and talking with the greatest Mevlevi leaders, the most influential of teachers, in North America and Europe.

They had met Çelebi, even travelled with him. And they had no idea of the treasure he held hidden inside himself.

To them he was just a businessman—nothing more. One famous teacher, in particular, was passionately telling me one evening how Konya is the centre for his tradition and all his spiritual work. When I mentioned a bit of what had happened during my meeting with Çelebi in Istanbul, he became confused.

Then he froze.

Early the next day, at the conference where we were, people started coming up to me with reports of what had happened when this man started giving his morning lecture. Later he, too, told me in person. He'd been about to open his mouth when he realized nothing was going to come out.

Suddenly he was aware of Rumi himself standing in the room, gagging him, grabbing his throat. And the lecture time was spent in silence almost until the end, when Rumi released his grip long enough for the teacher to speak a few stammering words.

Of course everything, after the horror of such an experience, soon returns to normal. It always does because, whatever our line of work or speciality, it has to so that the show can go on. If something bursts in from another reality, that's a regrettable embarrassment to recover from as quickly as possible; to rationalize away with our skilful choice of labels and words so we can keep clinging to the thread of what's most familiar by breaking the thread of the sacred.

And, of course, this is a problem for everyone without exception because we all need continuity so we at least can seem to function. But even those of us who think we're most awake are so easily lulled asleep by the sweet lullaby of routine—never quite able to take the next steps needed.

I did end up stopping in Konya, and did just as Çelebi recommended. The morning after I arrived, I went straight to join the crowds of pilgrims who were lined up waiting to pray and pay their respects at Rumi's tomb. Ahead of me, I could already see the exquisite drapings and almost taste inside my mouth the intoxicating aroma of devotion.

But just as I was about to reach it, was almost right in front of it, suddenly a voice seemed to speak out to me from inside the tomb—saying "Go to Shams!"

So I left; asked around in town; was told there is a special mosque, not far away, for Rumi's famous friend and teacher Shams of Tabriz.

When I arrived and went in, the place was totally empty: not a single living soul. And I ended up standing for hours, motionless, in front of Shams' tomb.

Every day I came back and did the same thing. After a while the keeper of the mosque approached and asked what I was doing. In my broken Turkish I said there are no words for it. And from then on we would silently greet each other with a warm smile, a slight bow, right hand over our heart.

I got to know the boys outside and join them in their pranks. Everywhere—the streets, the shops—the city was soaked in the spirit of Rumi.

But what impressed me above all was when a young child would come alone into the mosque to pray. The spontaneous intensity of their devotions, the unbelievable power and purity of their prostrations, showed me what I'd never seen so clearly before: the imbedded human instinct for prayer.

It needs a lot to knock that instinct out of a child with all the nonsense we teach them—training them to behave in the way we imagine children ought to, forcing them to indulge in our own weaknesses, infecting them with our infantilism.

It can be strange now to watch how the utter other-worldliness of Shams' relationship to Rumi, the devastating effects of their union, are so often turned by devotees into the quintessence of childlike excitability and gooey sentimentality. But this is what Shams from Tabriz does: he transforms children into adults and turns adults into children.

Day after day for hours on end I stood there without moving. At the same time, though, something was slowing moving inside—and as for whether one is allowed to talk about such things, absolutely not, but as for whether there are situations where one has to, absolutely.

Often people assume that, in the consciousness of God, external things and objects lose their value. And in a sense this is true because, to reach that consciousness, all those things need to be given freely away.

But, in the reality of divine consciousness, the external never loses its value. On the contrary: its value is simply transferred from the outside to inside in such a way that nothing is ever lost, because there can be no separation from anyone or anything.

For most people this is something almost impossible to imagine. Ordinarily, just the ability to perceive something means being more or less bound to find ourselves separated from it sooner or later—then missing it, longing for it or at least some variation of it, wanting it all over again.

But to perceive something consciously from inside the ground or sensation of one's own body is to absorb it; consume it; digest it; unite with it permanently and never be separated from it again. It's like the harvester gathering in the crop.

Day by day the standing and watching and praying went on. Then one afternoon I realized with a sudden shudder that the tomb of Shams, which had been so full when I first arrived, was completely empty.

And it was not only his tomb, with the green drape and turban on top. The world—this whole world of sense perception—had been emptied too, like a tiny drop of water sucked up by the sun.

Although east or west or further east hardly mattered, I knew that it was time for leaving Konya. The physical steps were simple: go to the main terminal, book my seat on a bus heading out to Antakya the next day.

But facing the indescribable weightiness of what had happened inside me was another matter altogether. There was the creeping certainty that one doesn't dialogue, alive, with the dead and simply stay alive as before. To absorb, assimilate, integrate, so much power from the dead by removing it from its tomb—I just might, if I am ever so fortunate, survive that and I might not.

This wouldn't be an easy journey.

BEAUTY

Coming back to Antioch was to slip inside the history of myself.

Either early or late to avoid the midday heat, I walked across the city and on to the outskirts; watched how two thousand years can evaporate in a single heartbeat; saw how different the reality here, but then, of being an apostle was from being some preacher or missionary today.

And at a certain degree of clarity, just as when ice turns into water, suddenly time itself melts away.

The only question worth asking was what could be more ancient, the city or me? The only answer worth giving was that it's all inside me—the beauty and squalor, the cave which once served as the first-ever church for Christians, the countless rivers running right down the hillsides in my heart.

Sometimes I was slowed, even brought to a stop, by periods of weakness. But they came with a certain grace, almost tenderly, less as a threat or danger than as a welcoming old friend. In my pocket I still had the name of the place that Çelebi had written down for me, together with the little map he'd drawn. And I was determined to find it even if this would be the last thing I ever did.

When you are in Antakya, Çelebi had said, I suggest you go there because according to tradition it's the place where the prophet Moses met the green one: the prophet Khidr who always appears in the strangest shapes and forms before vanishing again. There is a rock just beside the sea which is the sacred spot where all the opposites come together, where the two different strands of prophecy meet, where the invisible meets the visible, the extraordinary meets the ordinary in a secret place of healing and guidance that the reasoning mind even of a Moses can never understand—at the point where the two kinds of waters meet and the water meets the land.

So one morning I went to take the bus which is supposed to go there. Among the passengers was an American, roughly my age, and we started talking. He was heading in my direction but, like me, not too sure where.

We got out together in the town with the name Çelebi had given me, asked for the sea and felt utterly lost. People gestured as vaguely as possible, then got on with their carrying or cleaning. We walked down the gently sloping street that seemed to go on for ever, sometimes almost leaning on each other out of sheer fatigue.

Then at one point the determination of my American friend just melted. He'd had enough; turned around; disappeared.

In terms of physical distance it can't have been far, but I kept going for what felt an eternity. Then suddenly I smelled something: turned a slight corner and there was the sea.

At that particular moment another bus came rumbling down and pulled to a stop before getting swallowed in the sand. It circled a plain structure that presumably was used by the road repair workers for storing their equipment, and headed back up the way I'd come. Wearily I laughed to myself. If only I had stayed on my bus all the way to the end of the route, I would have been here a long time ago.

I wandered onto the sand, down to the sea, looking for the rock. The shoreline itself was totally bare; no one, here, had the slightest interest in bathing or swimming. But occasionally people would stroll by on the sand— sometimes locals, also visitors in couples or groups. I stopped every single person who was passing to ask where is the famous rock, mentioned in the holy Quran, which is the place where the prophet Moses met the prophet Khidr?

Nobody knew. It was obvious almost everyone thought I was crazy. One well-educated young couple paused for a while to talk to me and said, Oh yes! The famous rock where Khidr and Moses met: we know exactly what you are talking about, but you are years too late. There is no point in looking for it here because it was dug up a long time ago and transported, hundreds of kilometres away, to the national museum in Ankara.

Gradually I realized it had all been a waste of time, useless. I'd been given the wrong information and that was that. Like the American, I gave up. I walked right to the edge of the water and, as an unthinking gesture of surrender, stripped off my clothes until I was wearing nothing but underpants—then dove into the sea.

It's always good to know when you have been completely beaten. There was nothing left to do.

The water was as calm and motionless as glass. But when I came back to land, things were suddenly far harder. The sand was so hot it burned the wet soles of my feet. I didn't have a bag or towel or anything with me at all, so I hobbled and leaped across the scorching sand towards what looked like a restaurant in the distance; went into the bathroom to get dressed; then sat outside on a step so my underwear could dry.

And while I was waiting I just stared at the white round structure straight in front of me: the banal-looking building right in the centre of the street where all the buses and cars drove round.

Then it was as if something woke up inside me. I got to my feet and abruptly was pulled towards the dome-shaped structure; noticed a thin entrance like a slip and had a feeling as if I almost slid my way in.

Hidden from the road and the swirl of traffic outside, a couple of old men were sitting side by side on two fragile-looking chairs and beaming from ear to ear. They greeted me and told me to go in.

And then I saw what the whole structure was—nothing but a round wall and protective dome for the enormous rock filling all the space inside.

Along with a plaque, describing in Turkish and Arabic how this was the rock where the two prophets met, there was a tiny circular corridor separating the rock from the outside wall which was barely wide enough for a single human. And its rough, uncovered soil was covered with women.

They were lying—all of them barefoot, head to toe one after the other, body to body in their circle, hardly an inch to spare—asleep. To walk around the rock I had to hop and leapfrog over them. Halfway I stopped and stayed, breathing with them. From their faces and clothing it was obvious they were totally different from the local Sunni Turks: much more like the Shiite Muslims from further east.

And I began to understand why most of the local people knew nothing about the shrine or, just as simply, didn't want to.

These apparently sleeping women were doing the same incubation practice that Pythagoras did, or Parmenides used to do: not sitting cross-legged in upright meditation but lying abandoned on the ground as westerners originally used to meditate, surrendered to gravity, asleep or in a state which is neither sleep nor waking, open to a healing dream or inner guidance, waiting to be made pregnant.

The perfume from the resin, burning inside little trays on the ledges around the shrine, was glorious. Here— quite literally in the middle of the road, unrecognized as always, unknown—was total peace. This was the house of surrender where everything, the loneliness and suffering and struggles, the aspirations and aching and grieving, comes to an end.

When eventually I went out, the two old men were still sitting beside each other and waiting. We got to talking about this mystery that's hidden, like everything most important, out in the open. And they explained that, to complete my visit, it would be the tradition for me to circumambulate the rock by walking three times around the shrine outside the wall.

I said goodbye; began the circumambulation exactly as they described. But by the end of the third time around the shrine, something wouldn't let me stop. I was gripped by an inner force that said: Keep on going for another half a revolution, then turn your back to the rock and walk straight ahead until you can walk no further.

I did as I'd been told; or to be more honest, my body did it. I really had no choice. After the extra half a circle, when I turned to face away from the shrine, there was only a huge sand dune ahead of me with not even a glimpse of anything behind. I walked towards it in a perfectly straight line, aware of how absurd this was and not expecting a thing.

As I came near the crest of the dune, I started seeing the enormous vista of sea and seashore stretched out ahead of me. The entire shoreline was utterly deserted, totally empty. But right ahead of me, in precisely the direction I was walking, was the strangest sight: a small speck, half in the water, half on the land, which I soon saw was a half-naked man.

I went straight up to him, lying like some creature on the seashore at exactly the point where the water meets the land. The lower half of his body was in the water and the top half out of it. When he became aware of me approaching he didn't get up or even move; still lying on his back, he just rolled his eyes so he could see me. He started talking and telling me his story, half in French and half in Arabic. He was an intelligent man and explained how he half wanted to be here but half didn't, was here on a kind of vacation that actually wasn't a vacation at all. His home was Jordan but he wasn't able to go back there and his wife, who was there, wasn't able to join him. His health was not good, neither was hers.

His whole life was an endless division. He was full of regrets, full of peace. And then a moment came when nothing was the same. He sat up with his feet still in the water and said that he'd told me all about himself, but now he needed to say something about me. He began rattling off some platitudes—and then, all of a sudden, his voice completely changed.

He stretched out his right arm and hand, with his index finger pointing to the northwest across the sea. And he spoke one single sentence which, in that instant, completely changed my life. All my half-hearted decisions and well-reasoned plans were shattered, and the life I'd comfortably prepared to live was gone.

The man's voice returned to normal and we went on talking a little longer. We both were staying in Antakya and agreed: Let's meet again. Then we burst into laughter together.

How can we arrange a time to meet when we have no clue what life will bring?

Things were not looking too good for me.

I was feeling sick and steadily getting sicker with a strange malaise I just couldn't put my finger on. With a peculiar detachment I noticed I was having trouble eating, even drinking. I wasn't the only person, either, who was paying attention.

The Arab with the glistening gold teeth who owned the house where I was renting a room didn't miss a trick and could see me getting feebler. There is something unforgettable about the experience of being watched in the same way an animal keeps eyeing its weakening prey.

And as a simple matter of survival, I sensed I needed to be heading further east. It's only in extreme situations that we stop all the normal nonsense of behaving like fools dragging our bodies around with us and start, instead, to become a body carrying a fool.

The bus heading out to Urfa made a stop so everyone could stretch their legs at what once had been a major crossroads along the old caravan routes. Traders were there, selling beautiful melons and I bought a slice. But I couldn't even put it in my mouth—while the day and the distances across the desert stretched themselves out under the blazing sun.

Most of the people travelling with me were Kurds. I'd heard terrifying stories about how wild they are but with their gleaming eyes, living on the sharp edge of life, I couldn't find anything inside me to be afraid of. They were fascinated to know why I was coming into their territory and, when we arrived at the bridge with the big signs saying we were crossing the river Euphrates, nearly everybody on the bus gathered around to greet me: standing in the central corridor, climbing on the seats. Welcome to the Euphrates!

When we arrived in Urfa I could hardly walk. I asked a taxi driver to take me to a hotel where I could rest and the place he brought me to, with its quaint central courtyard, felt immensely old. The hotel owner, a youngish man, fetched some peppermint tea that I tried to drink—but, for some reason which I didn't have the mind to analyze, couldn't even take a sip of.

My room was like an ascetic's cell: low ceiling and walls hewn right out of the rough rock. Outside it could have been close to fifty degrees during the day and my windowless cave wasn't much cooler at night. I tried lying on the bed but couldn't breathe and struggled back out for some air.

On the stone slab next to the old well in the middle of the courtyard—I couldn't tell if it looked more like a bed or a coffin—I lay on my back, looking up at the sky. And the most memorable night in my life began.

Although I was so delirious I didn't realize I was delirious, there was no room for mistaking the seriousness of the situation. A voice, strange as always, as familiar as ever, started talking very calmly and matter-of-factly from inside me: Don't move your body an inch but keep absolutely still, because otherwise you won't get through this. I did exactly as I was told and stayed motionless.

After a while, the same voice said: Don't move your mind even a fraction of an inch but keep it absolutely still, because otherwise you'll never get through this. And I didn't let a thought move through my mind; wouldn't allow even a shadow of fear or panic to come in; stayed as calm as the sky and found myself sinking down, a speck of consciousness, deeper and deeper into the ocean of unconsciousness inside me.

There, still refusing to let myself be dragged away into thinking, I was shown how not only each single thought but even every sense perception we ever have is simply the product of a lifeless machine inside us. All our awareness of our surroundings, of ourself, is nothing but the information thrown up by that unintelligent machine—and in this computer of the mind there is no reality whatsoever.

We live in this computer because it's, literally, the substance of our lives. We spend the whole of our existence swimming, although never actually moving, in this vast liquid substance of our perceptions and thoughts like fish in water. And as I sank into the liquid substance I saw all my life flashing, like pictures, in front of my imaginary eyes.

But I wasn't only being confronted with amazing details of events from years and years ago which, consciously, I could never have remembered. I was also swimming in the substance of every possibility arising out of each event at every single intersection of my life.

All that endless vastness of potential as well as actual past was utterly present inside me as I lay, illusory towel still wrapped around my head to catch some of the illusory perspiration, without letting my body move; without moving my mind.

Next, the liquid I was immersed in wasn't only the substance of my memories and thoughts. It was the seething red and white liquid of my bloodstream, and I realized that I'd sunk right into the life inside my body.

Then the voice said: In a moment you are going to go unconscious. But before you do that, you absolutely need to pray to someone for help—to the one person you know will be able to be with you more than anybody else.

There were many great and grand people I could have prayed to. I didn't because I immediately became aware that only one person could stay with me in this state. He was a man I used to know in London who was so uncompromising in his love of freedom as well as life that he would willingly go out into the streets and let himself be beaten up by police, thrown into mental institutions, drugged and electric-shocked to the point of unconsciousness, just so he could enter the closed world of those judged to be insane and bring them a scent of reality: the touch of humanity.

When I finally made my way back to London and met him again, I mentioned praying to him. Humbly, his face full of cuts and wounds from his latest beating at the hands of the police, he said: Of course, I was there.

Then, for hours on the stone slab, I was unconscious. The only thing I still remember after drowning in my own depths was travelling through a long and narrow tunnel. Finally I arrived at the other end—burst of glorious sunlight, exquisite greenery, and people who loved me while they were alive but already had died rushing up to welcome and embrace me.

Just at the last moment, though, a kind of invisible membrane made them stop and they said: How wonderful to see you but it's not your time yet. You have to go back. There are things you still need to do.

Getting dragged back into physical existence—almost, with a question mark, not quite—was the roughest experience I have ever had. I was neither here nor there; far from sure if there was still any place for me, if I'd be able to squeeze a way back in.

And re-entering my own physical body was close to impossible. Literally I had to re-animate it. Consciously I had to make it breathe. If I forgot for only a moment, the breathing stopped and I had to make it start all over again.

I recognized that I was dancing on the edge of death and dimly knew—it was still before dawn—that I had to act. I tried to move but fell straight off the stone slab onto the ground; started crawling, dragging myself across the floor.

Seemingly, every gesture and effort was taking for ever. But the worst part of the ordeal was that not-so-simple act of breathing.

If I didn't force the body to breathe in, breathe out, it shut down and collapsed. And every time I did manage to breathe in, I hyperventilated from the incoming air and passed out. All of a sudden each breath had become a lifetime and a whole life was being concentrated into a single breath.

Then something happened that, already at the time, I realized was infinitely significant.

Along the corridor leading off from the central courtyard I caught a glimpse of the hotel owner sitting up straight on his mattress, quietly reciting his morning prayers. I could have—and should have—cried out for help. I knew I was dying.

But with an even greater certainty I knew I had absolutely no right to interrupt this man's prayers. There was no way I was going to come between him and his god, even if refusing to do so meant the end of me. His prayer was more important than my life. I had no right to anything at all.

Eventually he ended his prayers, started getting up for the day and saw me sprawled less than half-conscious alongside the foot of his bed. He came over to me, told me not to worry. The pharmacy just up the street would be opening in an hour or two: they'll help you, I'll take you.

I knew that, this way, I wouldn't survive. Helpless, I wondered what to do and then remembered how Çelebi had written down the name of a person who would help me if or when I ran into trouble in Urfa. I asked the young man to search through my pockets until he found the piece of paper containing the name of Çelebi's friend—together with the government building where he worked.

It was close by and so I insisted that he half drag me to the place, half carry me. He left me there, flashing in and out of consciousness, laid out on a bench at the side of the entrance hall. Almost immediately a soldier came in, asked what I was doing, and the best I could manage was to mumble the name of Çelebi's contact.

He scooped me straight up together with my little bag, put me in his jeep and we drove at high speed to the hospital. Carrying me in his arms he burst through the double doors and I could hardly believe what I saw. A massive room was filled with waiting, crying people— women, men, the elderly, children and babies.

The tumult was indescribable but he marched straight through it all; forced open another set of doors and there was a row of doctors, dressed in white, sitting behind a long table interviewing patients one by one. The soldier walked right up to the front, lowered me onto the table and watched while they examined me.

Suddenly they were calling out loud for an empty bed and, as I was being carried away, the doctor in the middle of the row said to me in clear English: We can't tell what caused your sickness. There could have been all sorts of things that happened. But you are the luckiest man in the world to have been brought here because you are so totally dehydrated it's a miracle you are alive.

Another fifteen minutes, twenty at the outside, and you would be dead.

Death is not to be recommended.

Even so, when mystics from almost all traditions talk about having to die before one dies, they are not just making things up. We are too prone to foolishness or self-deception unless, until, our physical existence has been broken down into the finest powder.

And, besides, coming close to dying does have its consolations. As I started drifting back into a more stable kind of consciousness—complete with intravenous drip attached—nothing was my own.

My bed, most certainly, wasn't mine. The turnover of patients was rapid with so many people to care for; so little room. But my own bed was being shared even before I left. The families and friends of the patients next to me shifted my body this way, pushed it over there, so they had plenty of space for sitting and laughing and crying.

My body, too, belonged to everyone around me. I'd been given the strictest instructions not to try eating anything solid at least for a week. But any mouth in the hospital was a mouth to be fed—and I simply smiled when the relatives of patients around me pressed hairy globs of home-made yoghurt together with other delicacies down my throat.

When it was my turn to be released I climbed down the tall stairs to the hospital entrance, took another taxi and asked for the best hotel in town. The driver dropped me outside an impressive-looking façade and the faces of the staff dropped when I tried marching, or wobbling, into the lobby.

But the man at reception did sign me in—although while I was writing my name he kept staring at the blood that was trickling down my arm onto his pen from the bandage wrapped around the spot where the intravenous tubes had been inserted.

And I was shown the room which would become my home for several thousand years.

I was able to stay totally alone; undisturbed. The walls vanished, the ceiling disappeared, the floor was gone. All the centuries fell away and, night and day, I was together with the prophets.

It was the most wonderful, as well as terrifying, place where all our itineraries are finally dashed and our plans are smashed: where everything affects everything and even I in the present, to the extent that there is any breath left in me, am able to breathe with and influence and change the living past.

This, as the saying goes, is the end of the storyline. From here on, you either have no life or every life is yours. And as for what once could have been called one's own existence: now it's nothing more than the thinnest strips of paradox dancing and rippling like ribbons in the wind.

The first paradox for me was that, as usual, ironically I'd been tricked and brought to Urfa under false pretences.

My conscious intention had been to come for the sake of Bardaisan, a Gnostic who lived in the city eighteen hundred years ago when its name was Edessa. I'd learned absolutely nothing from Çelebi or anyone else about Urfa's past until, after those days in my room, I went downstairs and the staff in the lobby started explaining the history of the place reaching back all the way to Abraham—then even beyond.

To people who knew, glorious Urfa was *peygamberler şehri*: city of the prophets.

I can still remember, when finally I was feeling just a little better, taking a bus to the southern edge of town. I got off at Job's Well; walked down the steps into the cave.

An ancient incubation site, this was where the prophet Job had patiently endured the sickness inflicted on him by Allah without crying out or protesting or claiming anything for himself because he would have preferred to die than doubt God's will. A sign had been posted with these words from the Quran:

O ne güzel kuldu!
Gerçekten o, tamamen Allah'a teveccüh etmişti

Oh what a beautiful creature he was, what a beautiful servant!
Truly he turned his attention totally and completely to God

As I was reading the inscription I heard a tinkling sound with peals of laughter in the background; walked over and, beauty to beauty, was greeted by the most exquisite sight.

Kurdish women and girls were gathered around a fountain where they all had arrived with their empty water containers, joking and singing and dancing, wearing brilliantly multicoloured dresses that reached almost to the ground and made them look—as well as sound—just like birds.

I turned back to the shrine for Job and the man in charge came straight over to me, took me across to the old well and hauled up for me a bucket of the water that had been given by God to Job to heal him. As the bucket came up I had to step back: the water was sparkling and gleaming so brightly.

I didn't get a bus for the return journey to the hotel. I walked all the way, through the middle of the Kurdish quarter stretching from the shrine into town. People kept stepping out of their shops and homes to stop me; welcome me in; sit me on a chair or crate flipped on its end; offer me something to drink. They explained how all the houses and businesses in the quarter had come into existence.

Every one of them was in violation of the government building codes and regulations. Kurds were feared. They were hated. No one was ever going to give them permission to build. So when the offices closed at the end of the day, when all the bureaucrats had gone home, that's when the building began—and continued through the night.

It was a city alongside the city that kept secretly growing and rising and changing while people slept, just like this book.

This is a stealthy kind of a book. It grows inside you when you don't notice.

It has a particular tireless alertness of its own. Far from casual, never for a moment forgetful, it creates and then extends itself with the same attention it uses to write itself while even I am sleeping.

But to insert itself into what's left of the West, that's precisely how it has to function. As I saw back at the hotel while getting ready to let this broken old body bring me home, and as I realized during the nonstop bus ride westwards for two days plus one unending night from Urfa all the way to Izmir, I had absolutely nothing to offer to a world that only wants what's shiny and new.

What I was bringing with me was worth less than an old sack of potatoes.

Four

KNEELINGS

THE VERY first time that I met a Native American, I was twelve.

She was walking down the central corridor almost as if she was looking for someone. My relatives had trustfully, in a time when trust was still allowed, placed me all alone on a train out of Vancouver that would take me far into the interior of British Columbia where my elder sister—teaching the indigenous children in a tiny village—would pick me up.

As soon as the woman saw me, she stopped and sat straight down in front of me. That didn't frighten me at all, but what scared me was the familiarity of her strangeness.

She had the hauntingly impersonal look I recognized, at once, of someone able to see into another world. And the fear grew when she abruptly announced that she was going to be telling me my future—the whole story of my life, of this toss-away existence I was still so close to the start of.

What terrified me even more, as the train kept swaying from one spectacular view to another across the Rockies, was when she mapped out for me the mountain of ordeals and hardships my life would consist of. But the one detail that lodged deepest, like a stone, inside me was when she said I'd only meet my real life's partner and future wife at the impossibly distant age of almost forty.

Then she got up; disappeared. And what she said came true.

The reality, though, is that to experience the future laid out for you like fresh concrete is one of the hardest things to bear. A very specific kind of nausea goes hand in hand with each realization that the future is not some optional possibility, some remote alternative to the present, but is just as solid and close as anything now.

Then, time is gone. The future is as touchable as the most distant, even mythical, past. Your middle, together with your end, is in every moment because they are both already there from the start.

And when time is gone, strangely enough, so is physical space. You can be anywhere in an instant because every-where is inside you—although, as a two-legged human, you still have to live inside the brokenness of space and time.

The summer of 1995 arrived just a few months before I was due to get married and move, with my wife, to Canada. We decided on a quick, exploratory journey to see where we would live. Everything, so far, was falling magically into place. The government of British Columbia had been bizarrely welcoming, inviting. And even before leaving London I would be introduced, through a dream, to the exact place that was to become our home.

But finding such exactness in our physical world is hardly ever so quick or easy. The fact is that we would still have to wait quite a while until we finally came, in our physical bodies, to the driveway I'd already walked down inside my dream—on a small island, once known as Xwlíl'xhwm, which had been the sacred meeting ground for tribes from all around.

For now, we began by driving around the far larger Vancouver Island. The beauty of nature there was simply indescribable. And so was the indefinable closedness of people's minds, frozen into hardness or niceness, locked away inside their private landscapes. Whether awake or asleep, no one could escape the worlds they'd created for themselves and then imposed on the earth around them.

We passed enchanted scenery; visited sacred groves, peculiar towns, ugly little communities lying on the land like lifeless bugs. And day by day something in my heart grew heavier—then heavier.

Next my whole body started feeling so heavy it was difficult, eventually, even to move. In full consciousness, as we drove or I struggled to walk, I watched something I'd only noticed very rarely before: something you can only see when your mind stays crystal clear, your thoughts are absolutely still.

Thin black fingers, darker than anything in existence, were slowly rising from the depths of the earth. Inside my body they were steadily creeping and climbing into the abdomen, then the heart, then the brain. If you don't think or panic but are able just to observe them, they'll show you what they are—an incredible intelligence which is the wisdom of the earth itself reaching out and upward ever so insistently, yearning to communicate, longing to make contact with humans.

Give way to panic and you'll be sure you are going mad. Or panic gently and feebly in the way most people tend to do and you'll feel the dead weight of a nameless depression creeping up on you; invading you; sucking you down.

Then you'll run to your friends, or to food or drink or drugs or the internet or the latest movie or, best of all, to your doctor because you can't stand the touch of darkness. You won't even stop for a moment to listen to what you can hear inside the core of yourself—the call from another world.

I stopped: made myself listen and watch because that's what it wants. Above all, I refused to be frightened or shaken as the heaviness kept swelling from something emotionally unbearable into something almost impossible for any physical body to bear.

Finally we arrived in the lovely city of Victoria; found a quaint bed-and-breakfast on a tree-lined street. I managed to open the car door—but couldn't even find the strength to climb out of the front seat.

At last I leaned and collapsed onto the pavement, dragged myself through the little wooden gate, curled up under the swirl of birds on the pretty lawn and lay totally motionless between the blades of grass like a fetus until the evening came.

We'd planned to meet a friend in town but Maria ended up going to see her alone. As night arrived, I crawled to our room; collapsed in bed.

And the dream came.

I am opening the door from a shabby, neglected corridor into an unlit windowless room. Inside was the glint of something alive, subtly but rapidly moving.

Then I saw her: the most unbelievably beautiful woman, unimaginably wild and free in spirit, absolutely naked except that she wore her nakedness with more composure than the most elaborate set of clothes.

Her black skin was gleaming through the darkness as she half stood, half crouched in a distorted posture I couldn't understand—except that it made me feel infinite pain.

Very slowly but firmly I inched forward, determined to help as if there was nothing else in the world to do.

"What's the matter?", I called out to her. "What's wrong?"

And with as much dignity as her twisted body would allow, she cried back: "How would you feel if you'd been raped and abused for almost two and a half thousand years?"

Immediately, while still asleep, I knew what I had to do. Without any regard for her fear or mine I half knelt, half crouched in front of her until we were virtually face to face.

And, as calmly as I could, I said: "Even if it's the last thing I ever do, I am going to show you that there's one man in the world you can trust."

Then I woke up and even the smallest feather of that heaviness was gone.

It had all melted away with the dream.

In an instant I understood what the pharmaceutical industry, the entertainment industry, psychiatric industry, food industries will do their damnedest not to allow to be told—because so much of their power derives from silencing it.

Clinical depression, acute and chronic and manic and mild, is always treated as something to avoid; get rid of; suppress; destroy. You'd have to be crazy to consider the possibility that depression isn't a human disease but a divine one or that depression in humans is a painfully precious message telling the story, for anyone able to hear, of what's gone wrong in the world of the sacred.

Nobody dares suppose that maybe it afflicts those who are more sensitive than usual for a very good reason— because beings far greater and wiser than us, the beings to whom we owe our own existence, are searching for the most sensitive people to touch and reach out to in their grief at what humans have done.

The problem isn't the depression.

Our fiction of a civilization is the problem. Nobody cares to go down to the underworld any more—truly go down, not as some nice exercise in imagination but as the reality of dying before one dies—because nobody knows how to.

So of course the underworld has to come to us.

There is no one left who can bear to face, then keep facing, the full horror of how a culture dies once it abandons the gates of death and cuts itself off from the realms of the dead. But it never dies out without first being sent a million hints and warnings—which all the fools we've allowed to govern and control us will keep working full-time to make sure we misread and ignore.

One of depression's most terrifying signs is the way it makes humans lose any thirst for the things they are supposed to run around chasing. Instead, they feel an endless emptiness and lethargy; the complete absence of any interest or sense of meaning.

But the real source of terror is the way this fabricated world of ours has been so stripped of meaning one has to be an idiot to look for anything interesting in it to begin with.

And what's most threatening of all about people who get depressed is that—even if they can't quite tell what's happening—for them the spell of this excitable world is being broken as a voice of blackness abruptly calls them back into their depths, back to where they come from.

The more anyone tries to silence that call, the louder it gets. The more you fight to shake off the gravity of that heaviness, the heavier it becomes.

But if you can only stay with it—be patient with it, learn its touch and feel—it just might take you to the place where you realize it's not your own heaviness at all.

It never has been; never was.

There you stand the chance of finding what's always been asked of humans—or what humans in their depths have always been asking of themselves.

And, for all the brutal violence of their optimism, they always will.

29

E VERY STEP with any meaning in my life, I've found, follows tradition.

Eventually, that morning, we got out of bed and went downstairs for some breakfast. But then I sensed that I needed to stay on alone, for a few minutes, in the old-style conservatory after they'd cleared all the cups and plates away.

Sitting among the tall, leaning plants I inwardly knelt down again in front of the black woman so I could ask her: What can I do for you now, how can I help?

Suddenly, astonishingly, she was there right in front of me—exactly the same as during my dream. Asleep, awake: to her there was simply no difference because, after all, in reality no difference exists.

And she recited for me, word by word, the opening chapter of a book.

It was only a few years later, when I'd already given the book its final touches, that I discovered—apparently by accident—how ancient sacred texts were once created.

A goddess or god would recite the opening words in a vision, maybe a dream.

Then it would be the writer's turn to carry that spoken work obediently forward: take care of the rest.

Soon after the book had been published, as *In the dark places of wisdom*, a letter arrived from a famous stranger.

He was one of the greatest authorities in America on spirituality and the best-known writer, at that time, on how to nurture our soul through the spiritual understanding of dreams.

He'd read the book; been deeply moved by it. And as he was coming to Canada to give some talks, we agreed to meet in Vancouver.

I took him for a walk in the magnificent park that runs beside the ocean. He asked how I came to write such a book about the dark wisdom of dreams and I explained that, needless to say, it all started from a dream. As the birds circled rapidly overhead, he stopped dead in his tracks on the path.

Then he turned to me, obviously unable to believe his ears. "You mean to say that you wrote a book about dreams because of a dream?"

He had never heard of such a thing and I'd never heard of such a thing as doubting such a thing. I was stunned that he was stunned; and I started to understand a little, against my will, about how the modern American psyche works.

We began walking again. Thoughtfully he asked if I would be willing to share the dream that lay behind the book. I said I'd be glad to, and went on to tell him about the shining black woman trapped inside the room alone.

He listened as hard as he could, commented on what an important dream it was, and then snapped back:

"But you shouldn't have knelt in front of her. That was a mistake! Men must never kneel and subordinate themselves to the feminine."

I let his comment go, smiling inwardly at the irony of someone from the land of the free telling me with such uprightness what I should and shouldn't dream. But it was only later, as the ferry was carrying me back to our island, that at long last it dawned on me what had happened.

Just after my wife and I had arrived as immigrants in Canada, I badly injured my back. The immediate result was that I couldn't sit in any chair, however comfortable, for more than a minute or two at the most.

And throughout all the months and years I worked away at it every day, there wasn't one single word of the book I didn't type into the small computer that sat on a battered old wooden chest in front of me—kneeling, the whole time, on the pink woollen blanket specially knitted for my wife by her grandmother.

Right or wrong, I knelt inside my dream face to face with the woman who would then give me the task of writing a book. And I wrote every word of it kneeling.

This is the power of those forgotten beings who shape our lives without the slightest awareness on our part, who do what we in our smartness only think we do—and who cry, night after silent night, at our forgetting.

I was made to kneel, awake, because I chose to kneel asleep. But there is no need to kneel to kneel. It's quite possible to kneel while walking and standing, swimming, sitting, lying.

The attitude is all that counts—an attitude of stillest surrender to this earth which has nothing to do with the pompous virtues of humility. It's simply a cosmic, loving necessity.

What's wrong is not the kneeling, but everything else. For two and a half thousand years the goddess has been raped and abused, unnoticed, because everyone was so busy with their ten thousand other things.

At any rate that's the glossy version of the story: a respectable and palatable telling which a few people here, or there, might even be willing to believe.

As for the reality, though—that's a little different. And that reality can be just a bit harder to swallow because our endless distractedness is, itself, the abuse.

All the busyness, itself, is the rape.

Moment after moment the assaults go on, not in spite of but thanks to each noble intention. And it's not only that nobody lifts a finger or raises a hand to help. It's not just that everyone turns away and allows the violation to go on taking place, is far too absorbed to be aware of what's being done to her day after day.

It's that each clever idea, every elegant alibi, is the violation. Even the tiniest movement of vanity, or self-satisfaction, is the abuse.

Innocence is not an option here and there is no neutrality anyone can claim. On the contrary: the more innocent you insist you are, the more insistent your abuse.

Each thought you have, every time you speak, is another rape. Even with your gentlest smiles you are raping her. You can thoughtfully agree with everything I say but, still, you're raping her.

And when you go to sleep with your borrowed wisdom, all the clattering of your thoughts, you can rest in the comfortable assurance that there is no lack of others to carry on.

Enlightened discussions and enlightening debates, the stimulating conferences, exciting gatherings, are collective rapes. You are never going to be the most eloquent of speakers if you know that the only thing really needed is to descend alone—like Parmenides such a long time ago, like Pythagoras—to the underworld, is to go down into the silent depths of yourself to listen and wait and learn.

To do that wasn't ever easy. Even in their own lifetimes Pythagoras, Empedocles, Parmenides, their immediate successors, had to face exile and the most total aloneness; massacre, torture. Then came all the torture, once the cleverest thinkers the West has supposedly ever known arrived on the scene, of what they'd taught.

Ever so politely, with a civilized laugh, Parmenides and his teachings were murdered. The logic he'd been given by the goddess of the underworld via visions and dreams was promptly replaced by a logic that, then the same as now, rejects whoever accepts such nonsense about goddesses or visions or dreams as empty-minded nobodies.

And, as simple as that, the exquisitely delicate teaching she created to help keep the path clear between her world and this world had been changed into a godsent excuse to block off the path for good.

Any notion that darkness could be a source of her wisdom, any wisdom, was officially cut off. But no one seemed to realize that distorting her messages, killing her messengers, wasn't just mindlessly unwise.

It was also the directest violation of the goddess who'd sent them: queen of the dead.

Out of sheerest stupid greed we snatched away the gifts so freely given by Persephone, who holds the whole world on her lap, and locked her up alone in a tiny room; twisted the dark and infinitely feminine mystery of logic into a vicious instrument for mental domination and control; fabricated all the miracles of modern education by becoming serial abusers of her little children from the very first moments they are sent to school.

In the violence of this abuse there are no nice histories of evolution, no satisfying timelines of progress. You could travel a hundred years without ever coming to an end of the grief for what this culture could have been—because there has never been any true history of the West aside from the history of her silence.

All our finest ideas about what to do are nothing but the politest excuses for hiding further and further away from that violation of the sacred. Every discussion about the future of our culture is just one more failure to understand that it was already over almost from the start.

And if this sounds like prophecy, that's because prophecy is precisely what it is.

Of course there are those who will say: We have so much to live for. There is so much in this world worth enjoying, worth trying to do.

That was perfectly true, once. But there is a moment and a place for everything. And now is the moment for folding, like nomads, the blanket of this culture; tidying up the loose ends; tucking in the corners.

Soon it will be time for moving on.

O N O U R I S L A N D we found paradise.

The house we'd been shown, then given, in dreams stood tall as a cathedral with its hundred and ten windows above the lake. And there was no need to go to nature. Nature came.

The deer prayed in front of us, facing motionless towards the sun, when they came out to shake off the winter; snored right underneath us as we sat outside in the summer heat; became perfect teachers in the secret art of fear.

Trees gave their shape and structure to the books I was asked to write. The glistening green-backed swallows offered words while the red-winged blackbirds showed how to let them fly, and cry, together. Eagles always visited, unfailing, in our times of intensest need.

Then the raven arrived, on 8 September 2001, to warn me about all the unending death and destruction lying just ahead. Before, I'd learned how to understand the birds by letting them take me into their world. But this was the first time I was forced into the gut-wrenching experience of having to decipher every part of its call and translate it into English, sound by sound, word by word.

We didn't need to wait for the raven to come, though, to know we'd have to leave. Paradise or not, there is the work that has to be done. Years earlier, I'd dreamt of having to plant grapevines across the whole of North America—being shown how such a task has to be managed plus the incalculable cost involved.

And besides: this tradition I'd been tricked into living for always works by travelling in a circle, then smaller circles inside the circle, around the land. In our case it was a circle that would take us from British Columbia through New Mexico, California, Georgia, North Carolina before returning us to Europe.

But I suppose, for the sake of some distant reader, I should make a couple of things clear.

This circling of the land is quite literal and intensely physical. At the same time, though, it's also a symbol: the visible gesture towards another, much richer reality. In other words it's far more than it seems—because behind the geography that we've agreed to believe in, of maps and continents and countries, there is another geography entirely.

We all glimpse that other geography for brief moments, before dismissing it as an illusion, because it's the geography of the soul.

There, the places we convince ourselves are half a world apart are separated by no more than half a dozen steps; and that place you normally consider just around the corner belongs in a different reality altogether.

There, you learn that physical distance is itself an illusion because you can be anywhere or everywhere in the blink of an eye. And you start to notice how everything is almost soundlessly, subtly, changing.

No maps exist on earth which are able to show the tides of life invisibly sweeping around and inside us, below and above. Sizes or distances that seem constant, to us, are constantly shifting. The proudest and loudest countries that once were massively significant can shrink into utter insignificance as soon as the silent reality of the space inside us has been ignored, misused, distorted long enough.

And on the level of the soul everything is always moving towards, then into, its opposite. What used to be places of freedom end up being turned into prisons—although of course their inhabitants naively go on believing they are free while still dreaming of freeing others.

Entire continents are reduced, along with the whole magnificent grandeur of their nature, to a space even smaller than some tiny island. And it's simply a matter of course that at the start or at the end of every culture this all has to be measured, inspected, recorded for the sake of the life to come.

Then there are the grapevines.

We live in such a peculiarly superficial world that we imagine any real work of teaching means teaching people. Usually we tend to assume it has to do with training people's minds—or, if not, awakening their deeper selves.

But that's always the least of it.

Grapevines are not planted in the mind—or anywhere else, for that matter, except the earth. And that's what this particular tradition is concerned with.

Of course people, too, have the earth inside them where they as individuals don't exist; and if you reach down into their darkest depths you touch the earth. You can be talking to an audience of hundreds in a hall and still, if you know what you're doing, are simply talking to the earth.

But as for trying to change a person's mind, or provide some handy tools for waking up: that's always the most trivial, most insignificant, part of any genuine teaching. It will never be anything more than a mildly useful diversion or distraction—a distraction just as risky for the teacher as for those being taught.

In reality, taking on the task of teaching people has for centuries been the worst imaginable way of helping them. And, completely unknown to the busy industry of modern spirituality, there is the truth that used to be spoken about but was forgotten long ago.

Growing up from the deepest region inside each of us like a weed is a fake existence, a counterfeit spirit, that takes the greatest care to force us to forget what we are and confuse us into thinking we are what we aren't. Right from the start it throws us off the scent, creates and shapes a perfect copy of our soul that faithfully imitates each single one of our best intentions, fakes our aspirations, takes every last drop of our energy and robs us of our longing, then pretends it wants to wake up.

And to understand this as it deserves to be understood is to realize that nearly all the spiritual discipline most people engage in under some teacher's well-intentioned guidance isn't having even the remotest genuine effect on them.

It's nourishing, then multiplying, that weed inside them: awakening their fakeness.

There is just one remedy for this—which is to return people to their brokenness. The problem is that, even then, they simply have to look away for the quickest moment and their brokenness will have been shifted into its opposite; only have to stumble onto something true and their counterfeit spirit will instantaneously strip it of its truth.

And so my main focus in human affairs isn't on helping people, but on helping the helpers. Much like Shams of Tabriz, I'm obliged to watch over those who claim to be the guides and teachers: keep an eye on them, a hand on their pulse.

The worst disturbances of all always lie where we least expect. The greatest danger—it's standing right beside you. To break through even a few of the smallest obstacles created by the most ordinary, most modest, assumptions is almost impossible.

And one has to be willing to walk straight into a concentration camp just for the sake of meeting with friends.

MEETINGS

31

I T C A N B E quite a thrill to think of being with Native Americans.

There are plenty of people eager to learn to dance and dress and drum; all the tribes of anthropologists with their exotic carved masks of objectivity; the guilty do-gooders desperately hoping, with a little bit of this or that, to be able to wipe away any trace of the trails of tears.

But everybody knows that's not enough. Something completely different has to come from somewhere else entirely. And every effort is utterly useless unless first we've learned to sing the song of our own indigenous reality— our primordial nature.

Each single time I encountered indigenous people in the United States, it was a mystery. I was called, they were called, and we came together exactly where we had been called to. There was the Tiwa elder who walked into an enormous room where I was sitting with my back to the door and, of all the places he could have walked to, felt moved to ask if he could sit right next to me.

Then he explained how, the instant he'd caught sight of me from behind, he immediately recognized who I was.

You are Coyote, he repeated. There is no need for you to introduce yourself or say a word, as I already know you.

You'll never be recognized or acknowledged in your own culture, because white people have no concept and no notion of what or who you are. You will always be treated badly and disrespected. They'll try to ignore you because they fear you; force you to live on the fringes even though, in the most fundamental sense, yours is the central role of all.

What they don't realize is that you are the bringer of gifts from the world which is our source. You are the origin of true creativity, of everything that's newest and most needed.

Few people are aware that only thanks to Coyote are they even able to continue or survive. And even fewer are willing to listen to his challenges or warnings.

But through our ancestors and our ancient ways, we still remember and understand.

Then, when life eventually took the two of us to North Carolina, it was a Cherokee medicine woman who came into my life.

She and I met at a big church in Asheville where we were supposed to be speaking at an event—not because either of us had the slightest wish to be there but because inwardly we both had been forced to come.

Across the huge hall I saw the tiny woman and intuitively knew that, out of all the people there, I only needed to talk with her. And when we went off to sit alone together in a little room behind the stage, Grandmother Red Leaf began by saying:

I know nothing about you and don't have any clue who you are, where you come from, what you do. But I was intensely aware of you from the first moment you came in through the door; and I knew exactly who you are by the way you walked.

The entire time you were moving across the floor in my direction, I saw you walking towards me backwards. Immediately I realized that you are Heyoka—one of those who work for the Ancestors. Nobody among your own people can understand you because you always do everything differently from everyone else.

But your work is vital and essential for the whole.

With the Hopis, just before the Kachinas or spirit beings come out: that, she added, is when the Heyoka or Contrary starts to dance. That's his time because he is the fool who questions everything and also forces people to question everything, for themselves, in the deepest place.

We discussed many things in that tiny room. Towards the end she proposed that we go out on the stage together, put our faith in each other, stand together. And after I'd shocked the pious audience enough with what they hadn't come to hear, the swell of anger grew far larger when she shocked them even more by reciting out loud my traditional names in the language of her own people as well as the languages of other tribes.

But just before we finished our little conversation, she revealed a bit about the strange chain of events that had forced her to come.

"I knew today was going to be a good day," she said. "Where I live, there's a very sweet bird that sings ahead of all the others before dawn. This morning, though, it sang sweeter than ever."

Then she leaned close and almost whispered the very same words that had been scratched and clawed into the grain of my consciousness for more than thirty years, morning after morning, by the birds. "That's extremely important. That's something to be noted, because the moment of dawn contains the whole of the day."

And most precious of all was Joseph—Beautiful Painted Arrow.

It started with us both being roped, as they say, into joining a conference in Albuquerque at a time when Maria and I found ourselves living on the edge of town. The conference was an impressive affair, Native Americans sitting in a big circle for serious dialogue with western scientists about whose learning could reach further, and tedious as hell.

When my turn came round for speaking, I gently protested that something was needed to balance so much grand theory. And as simply as possible I told the story of what happened when the raven arrived, with all its flap and flightiness, to talk to me in Canada—taking care to explain how sacred the raven was for ancient Greeks and how essential it still was, back then, to understand the language of the birds.

A number of the indigenous people erupted, either straight away or in outbursts through the rest of the day. One Yaqui medicine woman yelled at me that everybody knows the ancient Greeks and their wisdom are a pile of shit. As for the wife of the conference organizer: like her husband she was an indigenous leader from Canada and they'd arrived together in their shiny, top-of-the-line Mercedes. During the lunch break she leaned towards me and shouted across the table: "Who the hell do you think you are, you white fuck, claiming to know anything about the sacred?"

But then there is what they missed. After I'd finished describing for everyone present the humiliating ins and outs of listening to a raven, Joseph took the microphone and the magic began.

Looking me straight in the eye from where he was seated across the circle, he spelled out—minute after minute— the secrets of his people about the language and meaning of birds. The peculiar thing was that, all the time he was speaking to me, I was aware of two different realities.

First I knew that in fact he was talking to me not with his words but through his eyes and that if I broke his gaze for a moment, if I let one little thought pass through my mind, I'd instantly lose the thread of everything he said.

Second I realized that—of all the more than five hundred people surrounding us in the hall—not a single person would remember even the slightest detail of what he'd said because he had the ability, with everybody attentive and listening, to address just one person in a way no one else would ever notice or recall.

Later I checked as best I could. Nobody had heard a thing; and when I mentioned this to him afterwards, he'd laugh and laugh. What for us sounds impossible was, for Joseph, perfectly natural: no arrogance, not the slightest fuss, a constant sense on his part of utter nothingness and a gentler softness than the tenderest woman.

He showed Maria and me with finest precision how his tribe, without any assistance, always knows the exact time. He pointed out to us, in the blazing sunlight, the markers behind and beyond the visible sky. And, late one morning on his pueblo where he'd invited us to join him, it was his job to create rain for the ceremonies taking place that day after months of desert drought.

The dancers were waiting. Everybody was waiting. He asked if I'd come with him to bring the rain. Casually he took me to where his little old car was parked, still inside the great circle of trees marking out the centre of the village; sat himself down in the driver's seat, rolled down the window slightly and asked that I stand just outside the door beside him.

Then, softly, he began his ritual prayer. Straight away a tremendous wind came out of nowhere and started spinning in a circle—bending, twisting, the trees. There hadn't been a cloud in the sky all day, all week.

And suddenly a perfect circle of clouds started forming, out of nowhere, right above us.

Joseph rolled up the window, got out of his car, stood alongside me to say the job was done and now we'd better be moving quickly. Before we could take a single step, the water fell: no raindrops, no tiny patches of dryness but inundation as everything was drenched at once.

We ran back into the soaking crowds—Joseph just as unconcerned and selfless as if, instead of fixing the weather, he'd gone to his car to fetch a screwdriver. And this bears a bit of scrutiny.

If I too say or do things that may look or sound a little strange, it's not because I am crazy but because you are: crazy for forgetting what's real.

It's not that I invent or only imagine what I see. It's that I see and happen to hear what others might be too deaf or blind to be aware of.

We've made a game out of mocking mystics just as we love mocking prophets, but that's because we manage to make a mess of pretty much everything. Real mysticism isn't woolly-headedness or confusion—which are the usual qualities of more or less everyone else walking this earth.

A mystic is very simply someone who is three-hundred-and-sixty degrees alert in every direction, who makes no assumptions and takes nothing for granted, isn't afraid to look into the darkness everybody else ignores.

The ability to see into and then out of that darkness was, for Joseph, a crucial part of what he used to refer to as my medicine. Often he described it as the medicine of the ancient Greeks. And one afternoon he called me, out of the blue, to ask how I was.

I told him we'd been teaching in Europe and that I sensed my work in America was coming to an end. Immediately he said: "Yes, I could feel you were out of the country. You and I are one. But while I'm stuck fast here on this reservation, chief of my tribe, you and Maria are explorers. And I called to say that I suspect you'll now be returning to the Mediterranean.

"That's where this western civilization really began; and as every civilization comes to an end, the life inside it always returns to its source. That's where you will be needed next—so you can tend that ancient source, look after it, keep watch over it consciously. That's the way its life will be preserved and transferred, through the power of awareness, into a distant future."

Several years after Maria and I left the United States, we found ourselves moving into an apartment at the end of a small town on the edge of a little island in the heart of the Mediterranean. After a while, we learned that the name of the town in the local language meant "lookout" or "watch post".

And we discovered what those glistening lights were that we could watch over, from a distance, on a clear night.

They were the lights of Agrigento: the home city of Empedocles.

32

As always, there were outer meetings—and there also were the inner ones.

I only wrote a single book during all our years in the United States. The process began, to the extent that one can speak of beginnings, while we were still living in the mountains of north Georgia. I was sitting that day in our bedroom, completely awake, when a being whom I'll never forget came into the room.

He was covered in dust, from head to toe, with the feel of someone who's been travelling for ages without even stopping to eat or rest. He walked up to me, stayed still for a while beside me without saying a word. Then, just before leaving, he gave me the object he'd been carrying in his hand and that only I could see—unforgettable reminder of some ancient work waiting to be completed and of a primordial debt that needed to be paid.

It was a gleaming, metallic arrow.

Aside from its sheer unmistakable presence, it awoke vague memories in my brain. And as I slowly started unearthing the traces of this presence in ancient Greek texts—that's how the writing began.

One summer afternoon, a year or two later, I finished a small section of the book which soon would be published as *A story waiting to pierce you*. We'd moved to Asheville, North Carolina, and it was an afternoon I remember a little too well because it would sear itself into every cell of my body with a heat that doesn't even come from this world.

I was sitting all alone in our living room—reading out loud the sentences I'd just written about how people from the region now known as Mongolia not only helped bring western civilization into being but crossed continents to become Native Americans, about how Iroquois traditions originating in Asia shaped the founding and constitution of the United States, about how Americans with their imaginary achievements are just as unimportant as any other people or country unless they learn to experience the perfect interconnectedness of every nation and culture on earth.

Then it happened. As soon as I finished reading the last word, it was as if the sound of my voice made the floor of the room fall away.

Suddenly I found myself staring straight down into the heart of the whole cosmos as an enormous bolt of lightning shot out from inside it before curving, like a gigantic whip, and slamming right into my body in the room.

It nearly killed me. For months my body was constantly, if imperceptibly, quaking. Even now, no part of it works in quite the same way as before.

But inside that blast of lightning I was forced to recognize, at its core, an immense wave of expansive relief and gratitude coming from a consciousness far greater than any intelligence on earth. What I experienced as such a devastating force was also the boundless joy of something colossally powerful, caring, wise, waiting for this story to be told again—longing for the white people who have done so much harm to their little planet to be reminded of their right place and role in the whole of life.

Then I saw how even the greatest power in the universe is helpless, unable to do a thing, without the cooperation of what's smallest. It needed the feeblest and most fragile of human beings to cut through the web of human illusions; needed someone sitting right there, on American soil, to round off the circle of recognition by saying in a certain way and with a specific edge of awareness what had to be spoken out loud.

I'd never realized before that gratitude can be the end of a human being; or, in this case, a fate I'd been lucky to escape. But the computer which had been sitting on my lap didn't share my luck.

It was finished. The electronics were smashed, totally destroyed. And on, but mostly off, the record the technicians would tell me in sheer amazement—nervous, voices lowered—that the damage had been so complete it was beyond anybody's understanding or even anyone's belief.

Some time later an American friend, fluent in the traditions of Tibetan Buddhism, heard what had happened and was very concerned. She assured me spiritual practice should always be gentle, orderly, calm, and anything violent was to be viewed with the greatest suspicion.

It was clear she'd forgotten about the intensely ungentle, unordered ordeals the Buddha once had to go through. Obviously she also was unaware of how—according to mystical traditions in ancient Greece—being struck by a lightning bolt embodied everything that's best as well as worst about initiation.

You may make it through alive. You might not. There were no assurances, no warranties or guarantees. Even so, it was the purest possible form of purification: a sign of finest transformation through direct contact with the cosmic energy of the stars.

And at the same time it meant atoning, as far as anybody can, for the most ancient of crimes—meant helping in some significant way to pay off the collective debts already racked up by humanity long ago through its atrocities.

But this was only one of the ordeals prescribed for me by that book.

At a certain point as I was quietly edging along with the writing, helped by the occasional bear, I became aware that as a part of the process I needed to call a gathering of Native American chiefs from across the United States and Canada.

I had a good, long laugh at this new task being asked of me: it's not exactly the kind of thing white people decide to do on their own initiative. But then, obediently, I set about making the ridiculous happen.

First I did a bit of inquiring; came to hear about a woman living way out in the wilds of western North Carolina who'd been married to a Native American and was well connected. We managed to make contact, I noted down all the complicated details for finding a way to her cabin, and we agreed that I'd drive out to meet her one morning.

The night before, around dawn, I was visited by the most striking and vivid of dreams. Over breakfast I described it to Maria but we had no idea what it could mean. And because I had a long ride up into the mountains right ahead of me, I put it aside: forgot.

Finally I arrived; was sitting side by side with Diana on her sofa. Bit by bit I explained what was going on and could see her looking out from the corner of her eye, thinking what a ludicrous Englishman this is—imagining he can summon chiefs from different tribes and they are just going to come.

But leaving the matter there would, for me, have been far too easy. And soon I was laying down the conditions I'd been shown everyone would have to accept if the gathering was going to work.

There could be no room at all for self-importance, no grandstanding, no displays of ego: only the emptiest of spaces where we could see, without any illusions, the reality of what's happened to us collectively and could all listen together inside that emptiness and could weep.

Very politely Diana heard me out. Then she began humouring me—telling pleasant stories about Native Americans as if that was all I was after and no doubt hoping I'd leave after tea.

Suddenly she mentioned something in passing about birds, feathers, the importance of headdresses. I froze.

That stopped her abruptly and, when she asked what was wrong, I described how her words had shocked me into remembering my dream from early that same morning. And so I listened a second time to my voice reciting the dream.

Then she froze.

When eventually she started moving again, her voice and whole expression had changed. She asked for a few days so she could consult with people much more knowledgeable than her.

Two days later she called to confirm dates and details for the gathering. The chiefs and elders came from across the United States and Canada. One aboriginal elder even turned up from Australia because, at exactly the same time I was talking with Diana, he'd been woken and told he needed to buy an air ticket for North Carolina.

Just before the gathering began, Maria had a dream about it. She saw the full moon together with all the planets lined up, side by side, directly in front of it.

And she was told this conjunction happens only once every million years.

33

I T WAS STUNNING to watch the total respect with which the indigenous elders all came together and met.

Sara, a Mohawk from Canada, naturally settled into the role of presiding grandmother: the loving presence behind the event. When she talked about the great mystery it was the great mystery speaking. Where her eyes had been there was nothing but galaxies.

She gracefully laid out the task ahead. It would be a question of dusting the cobwebs from our hearing and regaining our spiritual ears; of using to the full the original senses each of us was given.

And never, she added, has that been more important because this time the circle will be different.

Before, it had always been the indigenous peoples who assembled to sit in their sacred gatherings. But, she went on: We only have a part of the answer and someone else is needed, now, to sit inside the circle.

So this is the first time in our experience that we are including any of them—she didn't even know how to refer to whites without being divisive or disrespectful—because we have to be done with the separateness and embrace the totality of life.

Formally she accepted Maria and me as elders of the western tradition; welcomed us into the circle. When our turns came round for speaking, we found ourselves talking about the wisdom of the ancestors.

And I emphasized that it's not only indigenous people who have their original instructions which were given to them by their lawbringers from the beginning.

Westerners do, too, because everyone is just the same: no difference at all. But whenever we tinker with those instructions, try forgetting them, think that we're smart enough to start making things up or tugging in all sorts of other stuff, then it's over.

Then we are already as good as lost—because the secret of nature is that only those with a firm footing in their own sacred tradition can relate fruitfully, meaningfully, creatively, to any other.

And ears were listening.

Early the next morning I was the last person to arrive for the dawn ceremony and thought I could slip in unnoticed. But Lloyd Elm—the Iroquois chief who had become leader of ceremonies for the entire gathering—stopped everything as soon as he saw me standing at the door.

With a loud voice he cried out: "The Great Spirit has sent you! It's the Great Spirit who sent you here to help and remind us." And he openly wept.

In front of everyone he confessed how, the night before, he was lying in bed agonizing over what I'd said about westerners forgetting their original instructions.

Then, too, he'd started weeping until his pillow was completely soaked through—not because of anything the whites had forgotten but because of what his own people had done, seduced into forgetting by the West. And he spent the night asking the spirit world for the strength to do what he knew he needed to do.

Later he told me how he'd made up his mind that when he got back to his people, the Onondaga, he was going to use all his authority and power to persuade them to change their ways. He explained how much trouble they created for themselves in thinking they could improve on the original instructions given to the Iroquois nations by subtly removing something here, adding something there.

And he talked about the urgency of never interfering with the sacred, which he realized he had to protect and keep purified with tears.

As for the westerners at the gathering, those white disciples of the indigenous teachers who happened to be present and watching: they sat as if they were carved out of stone. Most of them hated us almost to death; were so outraged at seeing Maria and me accepted into the circle of elders that on several occasions they pulled us aside to try dragging us off the property.

It was the same basic paradox I'd experienced in so many different shapes before—the chilling but also fascinating paradox of how I can say something about the history of the West which westerners are not even able to register while Native Americans instantly, wholeheartedly, apply it to themselves.

And this is because they still remember that they've forgotten, whereas we white people forgot ever forgetting long ago. So all we have now, aside from the terrors and confusion, is that insistent thud of a hollowness we can't explain.

Again it's just the same as with Persian Sufis—who were able to preserve and then remember and cherish the secret of the West discarded by the West for thousands of years. So, too, Native Americans not only remember their own sacred traditions even after being forced to forget them.

They also remember what we westerners have forgotten about ourselves: the fact that, for all our inhumanity, we too have our own original instructions.

As one Sioux elder once said with a big sigh, citing his own traditions as well as the prophecies of the Hopis, "We were told that we would see America come and go. And in a sense America is dying from within because it forgot the instructions for how to live on earth"—not anyone else's instructions, but its own.

Aside from that, there is so little left now to be said.

When the gathering eventually came to a close, the chiefs were as welcoming and generous as ever; talked about holding more meetings in future.

But much as we would have liked that, Maria's dream was clear enough. What had been asked of me had been done, what I'd been told would happen had happened—and then it's always time for moving on.

One thing, though, would never move on.

Planted, now, deep down in American soil would be the memory of two westerners addressing indigenous people from their own original instructions—and rooting that moment, along with the future, into the past.

As for the dream I'd seen, which was to make such an impression on all the elders that they'd agree to come together: I was walking into a public space wearing the most elaborate headdress of enormous bird feathers along with a mask on my face.

The thinnest mask imaginable, fitting with incredible precision, it was coloured the most brilliant and unearthly and luminous blue. And what was oddest of all about the dream was how absolutely natural it felt to be wearing a mask together with a headdress in the middle of strangers as well as among the people I knew.

But what had seemed so odd to me made instant sense in terms of indigenous prophecy—especially the prophecies by Hopis about a great spirit or Kachina whose arrival marks the end of our world, as well as the start of the purification that will make way for the new.

When the Blue Star Kachina with his coloured mask begins dancing out in the open, then takes his mask off, that will be the ending of everything familiar or old.

And it's the end because the energy he brings comes straight from the centre of the universe—from the heart of the whole cosmos which is the sacred place where each single nation and culture has its origin, its primordial home, in perfect harmony with every other.

This is the universal power that's needed to dissolve, then recreate. But it's also the cosmic energy which according to indigenous traditions is transmitted, on a human level, to the Heyoka: the simple contrary or clown.

And it's transmitted through the devastating power of thunder and lightning so as to shake people up; turn the accepted order upside down; ensure nothing remains the same.

The job of the Heyokas isn't just to get rid of everything possible. Ultimately, it's to make what's impossible real. That only comes later, though.

First, they come to undo what's been done.

LEAVINGS

L IFE LEFT when you weren't even looking, and now the whole world is old and grey.

Don't bother trying to touch things up and make them look just a little better. Your prettiest palette of colours, your passion and pride: they're old, they're grey.

We're so quick to suppose we know what life is, even though it escapes us. It's exactly what we think it's not.

It's not our heartbeat. That's only the remotest echo of what life is. And no one has any life at all we can call our own. We are simply cells in the body of a culture whose lifespan always stays a total mystery to everything inside it.

This whole world we live in, together with its future plus all its past, seems by definition infinitely vaster than the immensest jungle.

But it's not. Imagine a jungle and, in that jungle, a single tree. On that tree there is a single branch; on that one branch is a single twig; and on that twig is a tiny leaf.

The shiny, reflective surface of this rubbery leaf: that's our whole world. And everything else—the leaf itself, the twig, the branch, the tree, that jungle—is something we never get to see until we can step outside ourselves.

When I was living some years ago in North Carolina, my body longed to be able to experience swimming without the stink of chlorine. So I'd go to the Grove Park Inn where God knows how many celebrities, American presidents, have stayed. Every week I'd swim inside the spa.

And one day it all went very wrong.

I came in just the same as usual, sank into the pools. Next, I was there—but everything around me had gone. I was swimming in eternity: came from another place, another world, another time beyond all time.

Calmly I tested the experience, greeted the ghosts moving here and there. They were just a distant fantasy. Then I stepped into the bright warmth and lay on one of the sunbeds outside with people stretching all around me.

But they belonged to a different time. Their bodies, voices, laughter were as faded as the faintest memory because I was living and gently breathing centuries in the future.

They were all already dead. And the whole building, the hotel, the terrace, was just a hollow memory too. The only reality was the ruins everywhere in the open fields around me—small fragments here and there of fallen masonry, odd lumps of stone covered with wild brambles or grass.

And I wasn't just watching. I was, physically, the end of where I was. The present had become a figment and the future was all that was left.

Our ancestors still had names for this, or carved it onto rocks—while for us it's just oddity and lunacy. Mostly we are so slow, we want to leave when we ought to be arriving and stay when the time to go has come.

Life comes, then goes, as quick as a breath. You too are not here on your chair but out there in the fields of the future.

The trick is always to know how to leave when life does, breathe with it—hear the thundering heartbeat of eternity.

W<small>E CAN ONLY</small> have both feet firmly planted in the earth after travelling to each of the planets, one by one.

To visit every planet—that's not to leave the earth behind. That's wholeness. To have the chance to incarnate here on earth is crucially important, but to try keeping incarnated here all the time: that's a great mistake.

Sleep shows us this. Death demonstrates it. The destruction of cultures proves it. To be here, we have to learn also to be there; know how to come and go. To live as humans is to have the world of stars circling inside our head, the entire earth's surface in our heart and the vast underworld at our feet.

And only when our own name has been spelled across all the solar system are we on the edge of becoming those cosmic beings we are meant to be.

There was a time when I found myself being taken to different planets—once or twice in dreams, mostly awake. Only afterwards did I look back and realize the perfect pattern and sequence of the process as a whole.

Nothing had been arbitrary or an accident. Night and day were held together by a logic beyond my conscious knowledge or awareness. Still later I stumbled on traces of this same journeying in ancient Greek, as well as Sufi, traditions.

It's a reality untouched by scepticism, unscarred by belief. One's imagination plays no part; there's no place at all for fantasy. And the mind that makes us cynical is the first thing to be stripped away.

To be honest, the effort involved can seem utterly super-human. The demands imposed on each fragile traveller are beyond imagining. Even one's cells have to be trans-formed.

Every place demands new qualities of the visitor; each new challenge erupts as an astounding surprise. Out there in the cosmos, which happens to be the deepest depths of oneself, is where we see how infinitely inadequate and inept we are.

Even the finest, most sensitive human awareness falls so far short that life forms scatter from it and flee.

This is where you learn the meaning of cosmic endurance—where you have to grapple with how to handle not just hell, but paradise. It's where you start adapting to a reality in which nothing ever happens, and nothing changes, for thousands of years.

There you bake and ache beyond belief; are made to face the consequences, for us here, of how each moment of ignorance has repercussions through not just thousands but millions of years.

And you begin inching into an awareness of the real nature of life—spread everywhere through the cosmos.

Most of us are content to settle for childish fantasies about the possibilities of alien life; of extra-terrestrial beings. But in fact extra-terrestrial intelligence is raining down at every single moment on our streets and gardens and homes. It determines what we see; how we see; how we feel.

It determines what, and who, we are. It's us raining down onto ourselves: our own cosmic source and origin.

After all, we're simply here inside this little solar system to warm the slippers of our superiors.

It's what astrologers have guessed at but never reach, because they won't take the wool out of their ears long enough to hear the hiss and roaring of the planets all spinning in their orbits.

And it always happens now, and now. There's nothing more otherworldly to it than there is to anything else.

It's the mundane reality of speaking in tune with the planets—of swimming to shore, one summer evening, gliding through gleaming waters under alien skies towards another earth. That's the way life has always returned.

This is how the colour will come back.

IT WASN'T SUPPOSED to be this way.

Every episode from my own past that I started describing appeared, at first, with marvellous clarity. But as soon as the writing was done, the memory had vanished—gone, a void, as if it had never existed.

I'd assumed that the clearer I would remember these memories, once lived by someone called me, the longer they'd stay. But the exact opposite happened. Then it started dawning on me that if we hold on to memories out of longing, anger, fear, our emotions keep them alive and make them stronger.

When we hold them up, though, and watch them they just pop and are gone—forever.

I've been far beyond this cosmos, then all around it; seen the creatures that live on Venus; have known the love in front of which matter crumbles away.

And all that, too: it will fade, be gone.

It's the same with this ageing culture. Once, we served as midwives at its birth. Now I'm a midwife of its demise.

Whatever facts about it might be held on to by some future people will all seem accurate enough, and be nothing but emotional fictions.

To know how to bring things to a close: this is the essence of creation. My books and talks are meant to help you remember clearly—so you'll forget.

This whole book, you may notice, is silence.

I broke every rule and never even wrote a single word of it because I am behind all and am beyond all and I am all and am—where there's no earth, there's not yet a sky and there's nothing aside from silence.

I'm the place you come from, while also being obliged to play the strange role of being a very simple human being.

I am the one who sleeps forever, twin watchers perched at either shoulder. Here I lie waiting, so patiently, to draw everybody back to me.

Don't bother attempting to create some effect in this world until you've learned that kind of infinite patience. Try with your bright ideas to make it better and you destroy its fabric, tear it to pieces, rip it apart.

As the Greeks once said: listen to the flowers rise and turn and bow. Obey them, moment to moment. As Sufis said: Listen to the mountains.

Otherwise you fabricate your own destruction.

Get rid of what's unnecessary; of all that's superficial. Make your life a sculpture in eternity.

Let the birds etch their names into it—and the mountains shape it as they please.

NOTES

CHAPTER 7

The passage I found and read on the bus was R. Flacelière, *Plutarque sur la disparition des oracles* (Paris 1947) 258 ("fragrance reveals the presence of a god or a supernatural being"). See also P.A.H. de Boer in *Studies in the religion of ancient Israel* (Leiden 1972) 37–47 ("... the divine presence made itself known by scent, the perceptible form of the invisible spirit ... fragrance belongs to the essential being of gods ... god's odour, his revelation through fragrance ..."); A. Rescigno, *Plutarco, L'eclissi degli oracoli* (Naples 1995) 469–70; C.W. Shelmerdine in *The ages of Homer*, ed. J.B. Carter and S.P. Morris (Austin 1995) 103–104 with n.35; P. Borgeaud, *Rivista di storia e letteratura religiosa* 40 (2005) 595–600 ("... fragrance is a sign of the divine presence in all its immediacy ... in their epiphanies gods are perceived as a perfumed fragrance ...").

CHAPTER 9

On the ancient tradition of youngsters venturing into the desert see for example H. Corbin in *The dream and human societies*, ed. G.E. von Grunebaum and R. Caillois (Berkeley 1966) 388–9.

CHAPTER 12

For Empedocles on humans' inability to see or touch the divine reality, see especially H. Diels, *Poetarum philosophorum fragmenta* (Berlin 1901) 160 (fragment 133) = G. Zuntz, *Persephone* (Oxford 1971) 213–14 = L. Gemelli Marciano, *Die Vorsokratiker* ii (Düsseldorf 2009) 282–3, 420–1: "There is no bringing it near to ourselves so that it's accessible to our eyes, no touching it with our hands—which, for humans, is the greatest highway of persuasion plunging into the seat of their awareness." For some of the earliest pieces I published about Empedocles see *Ancient philosophy, mystery and magic* (Oxford 1995) and *Reality* (Inverness, CA 2003); also *Ancient philosophy* 22 (2002) 333–413.

CHAPTER 13

Proteus and the nature of seals: Homer, *Odyssey* 4.349–570; *Orphic hymn* 25.2 ("who revealed the origins of the whole of nature"); M. Detienne and J.–P. Vernant, *Les ruses de l'intelligence* (Paris 1974); P. Kingsley, *Reality* (Inverness, CA 2003) 239–40.

CHAPTER 14

For Empedocles' system of meditation see P. Kingsley, *Ancient philosophy* 22 (2002) 352–5 and 399–404; *Reality* (Inverness, CA 2003) 505–59; *Parabola* 31/1 (Spring 2006) 24–7; *Works & conversations* 22 (April 2011) 23–4. The book that landed on me fell open at the first page of a chapter dedicated to the seventeenth-century Persian Sufi 'Abd al-Razzâq Lâhîjî: H. Corbin, *Spiritual body and celestial earth* (Princeton 1977) 171. For what Lâhîjî says here see Kingsley, *Ancient philosophy, mystery and magic* (Oxford 1995) 381 with n.29, 387 with n.48; *Catafalque* (London 2018) 363–4.

CHAPTER 15

Henry Corbin never published anything about what happened between himself and Suhrawardî except very cryptically, which was the wisest of things for him to do (*Henry Corbin*, ed. C. Jambet, L'Herne vol. 39, Paris 1981, 46; P. Kingsley, *Catafalque*, London 2018, 367–8, 725–6). For Empedocles and Suhrawardî, Henry and Stella Corbin, see *Catafalque* 363–94, 723–68.

CHAPTER 17

For the language of birds and prophecy, along with the bizarre things that have been said about them and still are, see *Catafalque* (London 2018) 213–358, 628–41.

CHAPTER 18

For the details in this chapter see P. Kingsley, *In the dark places of wisdom* (Inverness, CA 1999); *Catafalque* (London 2018). I presented Parmenides' teachings, together with Empedocles', in *Reality* (Inverness, CA 2003). See also *Ancient philosophy* 22 (2002) 369–81, *Works & conversations* 22 (April 2011) 34–5 and L. Gemelli Marciano, *Parmenide* (Sankt Augustin 2013). On the importance of not changing anything see *In the dark places of wisdom* 209–10; *Reality* 55–9, 563; *Catafalque* 45–56, 216–18, 484–5, 600.

CHAPTER 20

Use of the word "child" by ancient magicians and mystics: A. Dieterich, *Abraxas* (Leipzig 1891) 160–3 and *Eine Mithrasliturgie* (3ʳᵈ ed., Leipzig 1923) 52–4; E. Norden, *Agnostos theos* (Leipzig 1913) 290–3; P. Kingsley, *Ancient philosophy, mystery and magic* (Oxford 1995) 221, 374 and in *From Poimandres to Jacob Böhme*, ed. R. van den Broek and C. van Heertum (Amsterdam 2000) 35–40.

For the crying and howling of prophets, see *Catafalque* (London 2018) 231–50, 274, 628–43. As Empedocles hinted: H. Diels, *Poetarum philosophorum fragmenta* (Berlin 1901) 150 (fragment 114) = Kingsley, *Reality* (Inverness, CA 2003) 313. As Sufis have known: see for example *Three early Sufi texts*, transl. N. Heer and K.L. Honerkamp (Louisville 2003) 47 ("The Messenger of God said: 'The people in the worst afflic- tion in the world are the prophets, then those most like them, and then those most like them.' The Messenger of God also said: 'If you knew what I know you would laugh but little, would weep much, and pour dust upon your heads,' and: 'He who sees God and His glory is in the worst affliction.'"); C.W. Ernst, *Rûzbihân Baqlî* (Richmond 1996) 85 (on the "inability to bear the weight of the calamities of unity"); Mawlânâ 'Alî ibn Husain Safî, *Beads of dew from the source of life*, transl. M. Holland (Fort Lauderdale 2001) 228 ("According to the venerable Shaikh Muhyi'd-Dîn 'Arabî: 'To certain saints, in the wake of their hard spiritual exercises, the secret of the apparent world is said to be disclosed. One night, I asked Allâh to reveal the true significance of this. I was shown something so tremendous that the back of the human being could not support its weight. Under the impact of the spiritual weight, my physical body was on the verge of being smashed to smithereens. I was rescued by imploring Allâh to conceal that inner meaning from me.'"); and compare Henry Corbin's translation of Mîr Dâmâd in *Mélanges Louis Massignon* i (Damascus 1956) 370–1.

CHAPTER 21

"The completion of all completions": *Pistis Sophia* 1.1, ed. C. Schmidt and transl. V. MacDermot (Leiden 1978) 2 (4).1–2, 4 (8).3–4. "The Father in the form of a dove": ibid. 1 (2).9–10. The edition of the text that I was introduced to in the bookstore was *Pistis Sophia*, transl. G. Horner

(London 1924). For the dove and God the Father in Gnostic tradition see also A.D. DeConick, *Vigiliae Christianae* 55 (2001) 234; and for the awkward uncertainties in the text of the official Gospels about how to describe the descent of the dove, B.D. Ehrman, *The orthodox corruption of Scripture* (New York 1993) 140–3.

On Gnosticism as orthodoxy and orthodox Christianity as heresy see P. Kingsley, *Catafalque* (London 2018) 146, 558–9. Gnosticism and Empedocles: *Ancient philosophy, mystery and magic* (Oxford 1995) 419 s.v. "Gnostic traditions"; *Ancient philosophy* 22 (2002) 339–52; *Catafalque* 197–204, 612–14. For words and names as deceptions according to Gnostic traditions see especially the *Gospel according to Philip* 11–13, 53.23–54.31, "The names given to the things of this world contain a great deception..." (R. McL. Wilson, *The Gospel of Philip*, London 1962, 29–30, 73–7; J.-Y. Leloup, *The Gospel of Philip*, Rochester, VT 2004, 42–7). Words and names as deceptions according to Empedocles: Kingsley, *Reality* (Inverness, CA 2003) 309–559.

CHAPTER 25

Khidr and Moses: Qur'an 18:60–82; J. Kreinath in *The seductions of pilgrimage*, ed. M.A. Di Giovine and D. Picard (Farnham 2015) 127–32; the site has been opened up and radically expanded since my visit to ensure as much as possible that, in the words of local tradition, "You will not see Khidr: Farewell!" For the practice of incubation see P. Kingsley, *Reality* (Inverness, CA 2003) 31–45; Kreinath, *Anthropology of the contemporary Middle East and Central Eurasia* 2 (2014) 25–66.

CHAPTER 27

O ne güzel kuldu ...: Qur'an 38:44; the Turkish translation used at the shrine was the one by Ali Fikri Yavuz. For Job's Well see J.B. Segal, *Edessa 'The blessed city'* (Oxford 1970) 54, 72–3 and Plate 38 with Qur'an 38:42.

CHAPTER 28

For Xwlíl'xhwm see R. Bringhurst, *Barcelona English language and literature studies* 3 (1992) 11–19 = *Howe sounds*, ed. R. Littlemore (Bowen Island 1994) 3–11.

On the subject of depression, James Hillman offers a number of seductive comments (see for example *A blue fire*, New York 1989, 152–9); but by psychologizing depression as "mine" or "yours" he never came close to the reality behind it. Of course nowadays it's absolutely necessary as a writer to make the formal disclaimer that one is not offering any treatment for depression, any guidance or advice. That remains the sole privilege and exclusive domain of professionals who must be allowed, at all costs, to continue exercising their monopoly over an exploding market by keeping their tables in the temple.

CHAPTER 29

On the equivalence of waking and sleeping see P. Kingsley, *In the dark places of wisdom* (Inverness, CA 1999) 80, 110–11, 245. For gods and goddesses dictating the first lines of a sacred text, the finest discussion is still the one by Otto Weinreich: *Archiv für Religionswissenschaft* 17 (1914) 524–31 = *Ausgewählte Schriften* i (Amsterdam 1969) 311–18. But compare also Friedrich Welcker, *Kleine Schriften* iii (Bonn 1850) 144–51. Weinreich reserves most of what he has to say on this topic for a section dedicated, very specifically, to the subject of kneeling in front of a divinity (*Archiv für Religionswissenschaft* 17, 1914, 527–31 = *Ausgewählte Schriften* i 314–18).

The murder of Parmenides: Plato, *Sophist* 241d–242a; Kingsley, *In the dark places of wisdom* 39–45 together with *Catafalque* (London 2018) 52–8, 489–91. The dismissal of "empty-minded nobodies": Aristotle, *On prophesying in dreams* 463b15–16 and 464a17–24. The discrediting of darkness: *In the dark places of wisdom*; *Catafalque* 47–50, 130, 486–8.

CHAPTER 30

A brief account of the raven's visit has been published in *ReVision* 26/4 (Spring 2004) 1–3. For the tradition of travelling in a circle around the land see P. Kingsley, *A story waiting to pierce you* (Inverness, CA 2010) 21 and 109, together with L. Gemelli Marciano, *Gnomon* 84 (2012) 39 and n.4. Offering one more indication among countless others of how incompetent most academics have become, the scholar Jan Bremmer misrepresents me as claiming that this tradition of walking in a great circle involved spinning and pirouetting while one walked (*Asdiwal* 13,

2018, 103–4). And it would be wrong to expect any end to such dizzying nonsense from those who insist on twisting the evidence like torturers— and who try so hard to refute what I write without realizing that what I've written has not only already refuted each of their arguments. It's refuted what they are. For the ultimate reality that academic effort gets absolutely nowhere by itself and achieves precisely nothing on its own see Kingsley, *Reality* (Inverness, CA 2003), especially 173–4.

For the counterfeit spirit, or *antimimon pneuma* in Greek, see *Pistis Sophia* 3.131, ed. C. Schmidt and transl. V. MacDermot (Leiden 1978) 332 (664).17 – 333 (666).14; C.G. Jung, *Psychology and religion* (2nd ed., London 1969) 177–80 §§263–7; M. Scopello, *Les gnostiques* (Paris 1991) 80 ("by means of appearances and the power of illusion it produces a complete inversion of values, transforming reality into a lie and lies into reality. As a result the human being loses all its bearings; starts interpreting its ignorance as knowledge; and gives up trying to pene- trate the illusion of the universe surrounding it on every side"). Like Shams of Tabriz: Shams-i Tabrîzî, *Maqâlât*, ed. M.-A. Movahhed (Tehran 1996) 82; *Me and Rumi*, transl. W.C. Chittick (Louisville 2004) 186; *Shams-e Tabrizi*, transl. F. Maleki (New Delhi 2011) 246 ("I have nothing to do with the vast majority of people in this world. I haven't come for them. I have come to check the pulse of those who claim they are leading the world to what's real").

CHAPTER 32

The significance of lightning for ancient Greeks: W. Burkert, *Glotta* 39 (1961) 208–13 = *Kleine Schriften* iv (Göttingen 2011) 128–34; P. Kingsley, *Ancient philosophy, mystery and magic* (Oxford 1995) 255–9; F. Graf and S.I. Johnston, *Ritual texts for the afterlife* (Abingdon 2007) 125–7, 206 n.54; A. Bernabé and A.I. Jiménez San Cristóbal, *Instruc- tions for the netherworld* (Leiden 2008) 111–14.

CHAPTER 33

I already spoke a little about the gathering at Mars Hill in *Works & conversations* 22 (April 2011) 29–30. "We were told that we would see America come and go …": Floyd Red Crow Westerman during an interview conducted by Bente Milton in September 1999; my gratitude to Rosie Westerman and Bente Milton for their exquisite help, as well as their permission to quote Red Crow's words.

CHAPTER 35

Travelling to other planets: see for example W. Anz, *Zur Frage nach dem Ursprung des Gnostizismus* (Leipzig 1897); I.P. Culianu, *Psychanodia* i (Leiden 1983) 48–54; F. Papan–Matin, *Beyond death* (Leiden 2010) 191. On the sound made by the planets compare P. Kingsley, *In the dark places of wisdom* (Inverness, CA 1999) 126–34, 247.

CHAPTER 36

Flowers: J. Bidez in *Catalogue des manuscrits alchimiques grecs* vi (Brussels 1928) 139–51 and *Mélanges Franz Cumont* (Brussels 1936) 85–100. Mountains: G. Böwering, *The mystical vision of existence in classical Islam* (Berlin 1980) 81.

To find out about Peter Kingsley's writings and work, visit

www.peterkingsley.org